NO-LIMIT LIFE

♥ ♣ ♦ ♠

DANGEROUS CONTENTS:

MAY CAUSE A RADIANT CONTAGIOUS SMILE, A JOYOUS MINDSET,

PROFITABLE POKER AND A WINNING LIFE!

♠ ♦ ♣ ♥

BY

CHARLIE SHOTEN

LEARN THE ART OF POKER FROM
ONE OF THE WORLD'S TOP-RANKED PROS

NO-LIMIT LIFE PUBLISHING

Text copyright © 2005 Charlie Shoten

Photography copyright © 2005 Pamela Shandel (*front cover, inside front cover, pages 7, 19, 23, 27, 35, 39, 49, 65, 67, 75, and 109, inside back cover and back cover*)

Photography copyright © 2005 Joe Smith Sr. (*pages 55, 71, 77, 83, 91, 97, 101 and 119*)

Photography copyright © 2005 CardPlayer.com (*pages 14 and 15*)

Illustration copyright © 2005 Corbis Stock Photography (*page 31*)

ISBN 978-0-615-12927-7

Library of Congress Cataloging-in-Publication Data available upon request.

NO-LIMIT LIFE PUBLISHING
Post Office Box 34298
Las Vegas, Nevada 89133

Every attempt has been made to trace accurate ownership of copyrighted material in this book. Errors and omissions will be corrected in subsequent editions, provided notification is sent to the publisher.

NO-LIMIT LIFE was written by Charlie Shoten and is a publication of No-Limit Life Publishing; designed by Nita Alvarez, The Alvarez Group, Inc., Los Angeles, CA

Printed in Los Angeles, California, USA

First Edition 2005

10 9 8 7 6 5 4 3 2 1

If these statements are not true for you...

- [ ] I live in the MOMENT more than ever before.
- [ ] I am relaxed and maintain FOCUS as never before.
- [ ] I wear a radiant contagious SMILE more often each day.
- [ ] I experience depression and anxiety LESS every day.
- [ ] I now have the best physical HEALTH of my life.
- [ ] I ENJOY myself and look FORWARD to every day.

THIS BOOK COULD CHANGE YOUR LIFE.

It's Simple and Takes Little Effort:
Just follow my TEN COMMITMENTS and let go of the harmful
memories, ideas, thoughts and beliefs you are holding onto.
See them vanish from your mindset and feel your freedom grow.

Consider the Risk and the Reward:
After letting go of them, you may fear you won't know who you are.
You may be disappointed again by having little or no results.
Or you may emerge as the strong and beautiful person you really are!

Your Main Obstacles:
Your fragile ego...your security blankets...your self-esteem...
BEING MORE OF WHAT YOU ARE <u>NOT</u> THAN WHO YOU ARE.

DEDICATION

To my daughter Stephanie and wonderful grandchildren Andrew and Alison: *I wish you well in all of your life pursuits. Accept what you choose. Don't complain even about being disappointed. Be true to yourself and love who you are more than any thought of what else you might be. Know the truth and love it with all your heart. Never replace what is real with anything else you wish for. Be brave, follow your own true path and remember my love is with you forever.*

Inspired by Elia Wise in *LETTER TO EARTH: Who We Are Becoming...What We Need to Know.* (Random House/Harmony)

ACKNOWLEDGEMENTS

To Elia Wise for *LETTER TO EARTH*. It has been a tremendous guide for me.

To Ihaleakala Hew Len, Ph.D. and Mabel Katz for sharing your hearts and your ancient Hawaiian forgiveness practice "Ho'oponopono" – to set us free with the keys to the kingdom of ZERO! I look forward to our next class.
Let the Divine Creator hold us all in His embrace. We are set free. It is done. I am the I am, I am all of "I". Behold the Light! Let it sing with joy. For all mankind will know. I am the Light. For "I am" the "I".

To Louis E. DeRosis, M.D. for your valuable time, giving me your best and letting me be. Thank God that your attention was focused on your own growth and development and not mine. That is what enabled me to grow.

To my sister Fran for always being there for me.

To my father and mother, Bill and Bea, eternal thanks.

To Julia Getskin and Louis Rosenthal, neighbors who made a difference.

Why This Book

THE NEW POKER entertainment industry is moving at warp speed and is grabbing the attention of a huge worldwide audience. Being in it from its inception, I have seen millions of people caught up in the new popularity of poker as participants and spectators. How many more millions will be drawn in one can only imagine. This past holiday season, countless people played live poker games in their homes, watched poker on TV and played video poker games on the internet. Poker is having a major impact worldwide.

I hope all of the people and businesses involved in poker make an extra effort to help create and sustain ethics and values within the industry. Let's do all we can to better the experience of everyone connected with the game – from employees to management, players to spectators, young and old.

A new business doesn't often give one the chance to do something from the heart. My own personal growth and future activities are intricately tied to the growth of everyone in poker. This book is my consuming passion. I do not have all the answers, but I know that I have found crucial answers for myself which I wish to share and which have made my life and poker experience one of joy and fulfillment.

I hope that *NO-LIMIT LIFE* inspires meaningful change, personal freedom and growth for people from all walks of life and that it percolates through each individual, organization and corporation touched by the industry. ♠

Thank you to James P. Owen for your inspiring book *COWBOY ETHICS: What Wall Street Can Learn from the Code of the West* (Stoecklein Publishing 2004; Ketchum, ID).

Contents

Preface

THOUGHT TERRORISTS (TT) are thoughts that cause hurtful feelings that torment us. In our culture, some TT – such as beliefs and ideas – are implanted in our minds by mass media, education, upbringing and peer pressure. Other TT can occur as a response to our own harmful experiences, such as neglect, abuse or crime.

When TT caused feelings of anger, hate, shame, fear, vindictiveness, resignation, resentment, jealousy, despair, hopelessness, anxiety or depression, we tried to heal ourselves from the pain with thoughts of getting even or retaliating.

This also empowered us to strike back at the person who hurt us and was our attempt to support and relieve ourselves of painful feelings. If the source of our TT were relatives or close friends, the hurt was magnified. When we felt helpless and unable to strike back, our feelings put us under tremendous stress, and like a cancer, grew in strength each day. This has a negative effect on every new experience, limits our creativity and blocks the achievement of the hopes, dreams and passionate desires deep within us.

Much of this neglect or abuse we never remember. It can be as subtle as a child's disappointment if a parent ignored a straight-A report card. We will never free ourselves from these feelings created by our TT, in response to traumas or more subtle experiences, until we let go of the thoughts we hold onto that cause and sustain them – feelings that are literally killing us emotionally and, in the longer term, physically. We must let go of the Thought Terrorists that cause them.

We are usually unaware that we hold onto these TT or that we sustain, nurture and feed them, hosting them as valued guests. We don't see their devastating damage. We never realize that we can let go of them and have a truly free and happy life.

These thoughts (TT) cause feelings that can impair, even destroy, our focus on our poker game and every other endeavor we undertake. Impaired focus prevents us from reaching our goals, and being defeated, causes anguish and disappointment that keeps us from being who we really are – living with a joyous mindset and a radiant contagious smile.

NO-LIMIT LIFE is my effort to share the Roadmap I now follow. It is short, funny, easy to read, enjoyable and perhaps the simplest and most effective path you could ever hope to follow. You don't need to buy any tools, take costly courses, adopt a new ideology or spend more than the price of this book to enjoy your new freedom.

Just read and re-read NO-LIMIT LIFE until you get it.
Then walk the path I use to allow my heart and mind to help me notice and let go of my TT 24/7, one at a time, so they can never again reek devastating damage to my poker game or my life. ♠

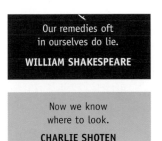

Our remedies oft
in ourselves do lie.

WILLIAM SHAKESPEARE

Now we know
where to look.

CHARLIE SHOTEN

No-Limit Hold'em and Me

I BEGAN PLAYING No-Limit Hold'em Poker in 2002. Although I have played poker since the age of five, I didn't know the essential skills needed to play No-Limit Hold'em.

One morning I read Phil Hellmuth's column in *Card Player Magazine* about why he laid down a Royal-Flush Draw early in a No-Limit tournament even though he was a slight favorite to win the hand. His strategy was to wait for a better opportunity to risk his chips. He was not willing to risk being eliminated from the tournament in that situation. From Phil's column, I learned that No-Limit Hold'em is a game of situations. You wait for the right time to gamble and risk only those chips in pots where your potential gain and destiny in the tournament justify your risk. Phil's column also gave me insight into when to play a hand before the flop and when to give up a hand after the flop. That day I entered a satellite at a Los Angeles casino and won an entry into a $3100 buy-in tournament. It was a remarkable event. All of my poker playing experience merged with this new knowledge, and for the first time I knew how to play No-Limit Hold'em.

With only three players left, Phil and I were at the final table. I won the tournament and $107,000 that day and never looked back. Thanks for your article, Phil. I finished 2003 ranked in *Card Player Magazine* as one of the Top Ten Tournament Players in the world with four wins, four seconds and 19 final tables.

My book, *NO-LIMIT LIFE,* explains in detail the Roadmap I follow which helps me let go of the destructive memories, ideas, thoughts and beliefs that I have been holding onto which have caused feelings that have been sabotaging my game and my life ever since I can remember. ♠

All of my poker playing experience merged with this new knowledge, and for the first time I knew how to play No-Limit Hold'em.

Thanks, Charlie!

What the Pros say about NO-LIMIT LIFE

HAVING READ CHARLIE SHOTEN'S ARTICLE, I sought him out during the Bay 101 Shooting Star tournament. Over dinner, Charlie explained his article in depth and was receptive to questions about certain aspects relating to his writing. After several hours, I realized that Charlie's article ["Play No-Limit Hold'em and Life"] was referring to living life to its fullest potential. Because Charlie is a winning poker player, he makes the logical connection to No-Limit Hold'em.

I always knew I could play winning poker, but something was missing! I would get frustrated and disappointed with myself, the cards, other players, etc. After reading Charlie's article and getting his personal insights, I began to put into practice his steps to achieving confidence, clarity and maximum focus on myself. By achieving inner peace with myself, the poker just fell into place.

I went to work at Binion's for the World Series of Poker, entered the casino employee's event and won First Place – $40,000! I had achieved my first win in a major poker event and now have a coveted gold bracelet I proudly wear!

Thank you, Charlie Shoten! Part of this bracelet belongs to you. There was no magical poker strategy Charlie gave me – just the ability to achieve my maximum potential.

Carl "Coach" Nessel
Los Angeles, California

I HAVE PLAYED POKER with Charlie several times and we even made some final tables together. He has impressed me with his confidence and especially his patience. It has always been interesting and helpful to discuss our strategies and give each other advice. I read Charlie's book, *NO-LIMIT LIFE*, and it really helped, not only when playing many poker tournaments, but also in many aspects of my personal life. I recommend his book to all poker enthusiasts.

Juan Carlos Mortensen
World Series Champion
World Poker Tour Champion
Las Vegas, Nevada and Madrid, Spain

M R. SHOTEN HAS ADVISED ME on how to play certain hands correctly for the past two years. One time he explained that I shouldn't get mad at a new player because he caused me to lose a pot that I had played correctly. He also explained to the new player what he had done wrong in order to help him. I have won two World Series gold bracelets thanks to Mr. Shoten's advice. I recommend you buy his book!

Minh Nguyen
Los Angeles, California

THE NEW BOOK by Charles Shoten deserves to become a CLASSIC. Its simple, clear principles apply to anyone motivated to succeed – not only to the No-Limit Hold'em poker player. Negative self-talk may stand in the way of success more than any other single obstacle for many people. The Shoten "Ten Commitments" provide a method for intensely focusing the attention on the present with a clear, compassionate mind while putting aside all doubts and fears. Insecure people preoccupied with past and potential future failures and disappointments can take new heart with the Ten Commitments.

"Thought Terrorists" (TT) became the identifiable enemy that the Ten Commitment techniques help to destroy forever. This framework coaches the reader in the unquestionable value of having a joyous mindset.

A whole new outlook can result by systematically identifying and destroying the insidious negative thinking of a lifetime of poor self-esteem. Gratefully enjoying the new, liberated frame of mind may have a ripple effect on others.

A wonderful potential exists, the book tells us, for the poker community to embrace these concepts and communicate them to others through the increasingly popular sport of televised poker games.

The principles of *NO-LIMIT LIFE* deserve study and practice by players and non-players of poker. The admirably short length of the book will encourage the potential reader. The concepts described seem reminiscent of Steven Covey's *The Seven Habits of Highly Effective People*, as well as of the meditative notion of mindfulness with focus on the positive present existence. The classic "thought-stopping" technique, developed by Albert Ellis, Ph.D., one of the fathers of cognitive-behavioral therapy, has similarities to the Shoten method of stopping the Thought Terrorists. A simple but effective intervention, the thought-stopping technique involves putting a rubber band around the wrist and snapping it against the skin while emphatically thinking "STOP!" to get rid of distressing thoughts. This might help the poker player suffering from intrusive thoughts of bad beats to bridge the gap until mastering the Ten Commitments.

The thorough reader of *NO-LIMIT LIFE* will come out a winner.

Karen L. Cruey, M.D.
Adult, Adolescent and Child Psychiatry, Psychotherapy,
Court-Ordered Assessments and Independent Medical Evaluations
Las Vegas, Nevada

THANKS, CHARLIE – for your article and the time we spent together discussing my No-Limit Hold'em game. We meet quite often at a final table somewhere and I appreciate your helpfulness in spite of our competitive play. My demeanor, and therefore my confidence in my game, is better. I'm finding myself at final tables more often and you have certainly contributed to my improved play.

"Miami" John Cernuto
Las Vegas, Nevada

MY FIRST REMEMBRANCE of Charlie Shoten was the catchy name he used – Scotty Warbucks. Charlie's old poker results were nothing out of the ordinary. In fact, I don't think anyone considered Charlie to be a very good player. Then, about three years ago, Charlie's mediocrity ended. All of a sudden, he became a powerful force in the tournament poker world. His results became extraordinary and have stayed that way.

A year ago we had breakfast together in San Jose. It was finally the right time to ask him why he seemed like a different person and how his results had so drastically changed in the last few years. He basically articulated what he eventually put into his now-famous magazine article, "Play Winning No-Limit Hold'em and Life". I resolved a number of issues that were eluding me that I had never even considered before.

My main issue was my EXPECTATIONS. Because I was an old pro, had done very well in the past and was well known, I was very hard on myself. I had unrealistic and irrelevant ideas about my play and these were all obstacles in my decision-making process. Charlie made me aware, helped me understand the damage being done to my goals and aspirations and shared his Roadmap with me for letting them go.

The following week I went to the Horseshoe Casino in Oregon where I was hosting a tournament. I kept thinking throughout that tournament about what Charlie and I had discussed. I ended up winning a tournament with 350 players, had two other in-the-money finishes and came in Second in the Best

All-Around Players' contest. After the tournament ended, I was convinced it was largely due to the advice I had received from Charlie. Since then, I slip a little now and then and forget to apply what I learned from him, but usually after I have poor results for a few tournaments, something clicks in my mind and I realize that I must go back and review Charlie's material. The bottom line is that if you follow Charlie's advice and apply his concepts, you will probably see yourself doing better in all aspects of your life. Thanks, Charlie.

Vince Burgio
Los Angeles, California

Note: Vince won the first three No-Limit Hold'em tournaments in The Plaza World Classic 2005 at the Plaza Hotel in Las Vegas on April 20, 21, 22, 2005, with buy-ins of $1,500, $1,000 and $2,000. [See Vince's "A Pro's Reaction" on pages 106-7].

I WAS PLAYING with Charlie in a super satellite when he gave me an autographed copy of his article, "Play Winning No-Limit Hold'em." Two days later, I won the gold bracelet and $136,000 in the World Series of Poker Senior Event. That's what I call an immediate impact! It was your article that made the difference. Thanks a million, Charlie!

I play the best against the best players only.

I would like to be your agent and find you a game.

Guy R. Gibbs
Los Angeles, California

I ALWAYS SMILE when I see Charlie because I know my game and my life are going to get better.

Scotty Nguyen

Los Angeles, California

World Series of Poker Champion

Photo courtesy of CardPlayer.com

THANKS, CHARLIE! I won my first major No-Limit Hold'em tournament at the Commerce Casino – and $189,000. I was constantly thinking about your Article. At the final table, "Be Present" kept me from going out on a limb and helped me stay focused. How did you write this? I never considered these concepts before. Please write more.

Sirous Baghchehsarie

Los Angeles, California

I READ YOUR ARTICLE during a tournament and suddenly I started focusing. Usually so many things are going on, but I went all the way with a new attitude. The negativity and fear were taken out of my play. I came in First in chips when a deal was made. I have a whole new attitude about poker and life now. Thanks again, Charlie.

Param Gill

Los Angeles, California

B EING A BUDDHIST, I especially appreciate and hold a special affection for Charlie. He's always making philosophical quotes. What's not to love? People describe his poker game as "crafty, sneaky and patient...a true gentleman."

His game gets better and better every day. Head-up at a final table with him, I smiled on the outside, but knew I had my work cut out for me. It felt a little bad to beat him...and a lot good, too.

Photo courtesy of CardPlayer.com

My wife says she loves *NO-LIMIT LIFE*. We read it over and over again and laugh out loud every time at the cartoons and quotes. Charlie makes Shakespeare easy to understand and agree with him...or maybe he agrees with Shakespeare? Either way, he gets his point across. As "Guru Charlie", he makes fun of himself and his student (who, by accident, reminds me of Scotty Nguyen).

We will continue to read and enjoy Charlie's book for long time. May it shine a bright light on the entire poker community. Unfortunately, it may also make it harder for me to win tournaments.

Men "The Master" Nguyen

Los Angeles, California

1996 Fourth Place, WSOP Championship Event

2003 First Place, Legends of Poker

2003 First Place, World Poker Finals Limit Hold'em

2003 First Place, World Poker Challenge Pot Limit Omaha

2004 First Place, Bay 101 Shooting Star Limit Hold'em

About Charlie

I DO NOT WISH TO spend too much time on my past. Thinking today about the past reasons for distress causes more distress, more wounds and even more Thought Terrorists (TT). Most of us are bored with hearing other people's stories over and over again. No one wants to hear that my mother did this to me and my brother or sister that. Stay current with what is going on with you now.

As a young man, I put all my focus and energy into sports, business and gambling. The area of my life that I craved – intimate relationships – I avoided. My efforts in that area often found failure and disappointment. I was not willing to risk efforts in that arena again. It left a deep hole in my being, but I was just not equipped to engage and I knew it.

All my efforts went into building up my self-esteem through the idea that if I made enough money, I could then start to live the life I desired and I would feel better about myself.

How will
I know if
your book
has helped me?

You will
be smiling
more often.

I made the money and then had to spend much effort and many years to get rid of it so that I could hit rock bottom, be hospitalized and be forced to deal with the truth about myself.

I was more of what I was *not* than who I *was*. That is where I began to get the clue to the existence and the nature of the Thought

Terrorists I was harboring. My symptoms were chronic depression and high anxiety levels. Like Houdini, I am now setting myself free one Thought Terrorist at a time. I am sharing my Roadmap that is liberating me each and every moment 24/7 from the baggage I have been carrying.

I label them Thought Terrorists because they are like the fanatical terrorists our country and the world are facing today. Both terrorists' only intentions are to kill us.

If we let go of our own Terrorists, we will live in a world with more love and compassion. It will be the biggest and best contribution we can make to the community of man. ♠

How do TT destroy my immune system?

Deliberately and with malice.

I WROTE THIS POEM as a very young man. It is the light that kept me on the path to eventually writing this book.

Perceptions of allegations
are not all right for me.
For who could find
through so much mind
a boy who has to be?
The sharks all around
are of nothing
but my own creation.
I can make them,
or break them,
or turn them around,
Even send them aground.

Three years after this poem
was written, I changed
"For who could find..."
to *"I will find...."*
On that day this book was born.

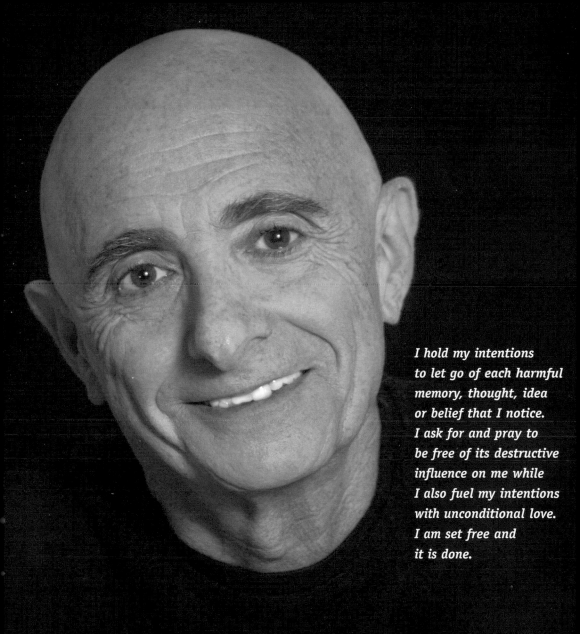

I hold my intentions
to let go of each harmful
memory, thought, idea
or belief that I notice.
I ask for and pray to
be free of its destructive
influence on me while
I also fuel my intentions
with unconditional love.
I am set free and
it is done.

My Roadmap to Freedom

MY MAGAZINE ARTICLE (page 26) is my Roadmap to a radiant contagious smile and to freedom from the constant struggle to build up and support my self-esteem. It empowers me to place more trust in my feelings and in my decision-making process.

I am the ultimate freedom-fighter. I want to be all of who I am and none of what I am not. Any harmful thought, belief or idea that I hold is

What have I been doing wrong all my life?

You have been yearning for something and then TRYING to get it. Please don't TRY to let go of TRYING.

vulnerable at all times. If I notice it creating stress, I let go of it. This is a good death for any parasite or terrorist. If I find a Thought Terrorist within, it is history. My Ten Commitments are working for me 24/7 like a perpetual engine weakening my attachment to them and helping me let go of them.

> Fiend! Most credulous fool, egregious murderer, thief, any thing that's due to all the villains past, in being to come.
>
> **WILLIAM SHAKESPEARE**

> Well said.
>
> **CHARLIE SHOTEN**

"Beware HARD-TO-DO, TRYING, PREJUDICE, SELF-DOUBT, DEMANDS, JUDGMENTS and any other Thought Terrorists I notice and name. You are history when I find you!"

How long will it take to be free of my Thought Terrorists?

As soon as you notice TRYING, EXPECTATIONS, HARD TO DO or any other TT and you let go of them

I am passing my Roadmap on to those who also see themselves as prisoners of self-imposed Thought Terrorists. My Roadmap is the opposite of what is taught in our schools and institutions. Positive thinking can sometimes be more destructive than negative thinking because it appears as a good force and not as the deceiving terrorist it can potentially be.

I TRY so hard to say goodbye to HARD TO DO and TRYING, but they never say goodbye to me.

Don't you see what you are saying?

All experiences are different, of course, but in my case, I missed the effects the Thought Terrorist forces had on me. With an enormous effort of positive thinking, I tried to accomplish a lot of things, but was often met with such terrible and humiliating defeat (in my eyes), that it drove me deeper into isolation and built up my Thought Terrorist network which really was quite a fascist internal force.

All that we are is the result of what we have thought, what we think, we become.

MAHARISHI MAHESH YOGI

Now we have the Roadmap and are equipped to let go of those thoughts that are destroying us.

CHARLIE SHOTEN

I now promote my Roadmap everywhere, especially emphasizing being present in the moment, being who you really are and having a joyous mindset and a radiant contagious smile.

We must focus on being less of what we are not in order to be who we already are. We all are already the all of the all of who we are, who we can be, what destiny has in store for us and the purest of love found anywhere.

Humanity is a great blessing. Let's celebrate and embrace ever so gently and kindly our common humanity. This is hard to argue with, so help me spread my message. The greatest news I am sharing with you is the straightest, simplest and easiest road to that radiant contagious smile that you could ever hope for. You who think that being present in the moment and being who you really are is not worthwhile should not spend your time reading this book. Come back to it if you change your mind.

> To grow, be willing to let your present be totally unlike your past. Your history is not your destiny.
>
> **ALLAN COHEN**

> To grow or not to grow: That is the question.
>
> **CHARLIE SHOTEN**

We create Thought Terrorists and hold onto them in reaction to hurtful experiences. Remembering and reliving painful experiences recreates the Thought Terrorists that cause feelings such as resentment, contempt, resignation and vindictiveness.

If we could see how much TT baggage we carry, we would be overwhelmed. Here's a simple process that has helped me free myself from TT once they are in my sight. Compare going to the emergency room to have a surgeon save you from a bullet wound to a visit with a mental health counselor to free you from depression and high anxieties. If the surgeon

When you say "Become LESS of what you are NOT", what do you really mean?

Notice each TT, such as RESENTMENT or CONTEMPT, as it appears, and keep my Ten Commitments in the forefront of your mindset. Your INTENTIONS within will then allow you to easily let go of them.

Each moment is new and to be perceived as a clean slate. You will always be able to make your best choice in poker and in your life.

My psychiatrist tells me I should get to know myself a lot better.

I suggest that you get to know what it is that you are holding onto that you are not a lot better... a shift in insight.

asks you for the caliber of the bullet, you might bleed to death before he could operate and save you. Asking you to go back into your past and discuss all of the reasons and circumstances that caused your anxieties and depression is like asking about the caliber of the bullet. Reliving your hurtful experiences will create more wounds and more TT and you will never free yourself from this unending cycle. Being present and experiencing what is going on with you in the current moment is the only path to free yourself from the TT that you need to notice and let go of. You can never change the experience of those past traumas in your life, so don't go there.

The TT that you are holding onto are like political terrorists who hold you hostage and threaten to behead you. What does the U.S. military do to get rid of their political terrorists? 95% of their effort goes into finding them. It is called intelligence. Once they are located, a missile can be sent to destroy any terrorist anywhere anytime.

> Man will occasionally stumble over the truth, but usually manages to pick himself up, walk over or around it, and carry on.
>
> **WINSTON CHURCHILL**

> Why not embrace the truth if it is destroying you? You won't stumble and need to be picked up.
>
> **CHARLIE SHOTEN**

> Change your thoughts and you change your world.
>
> **HAROLD R. MCLINDON**

> Let go of any stressful thought you hold and you will enjoy the world you already have.
>
> **CHARLIE SHOTEN**

Just like the U.S. military, we need to spend our efforts focusing on finding or noticing TT that we may have right before our eyes, but have never had the awareness of what they really are and the terrible damage they do to our lives through the hurtful feelings they cause. And with our new perception and our Ten Commitments, we can now quietly wait for TT to appear, then focus our intentions to help us let go of them so they cannot hurt us again.

Gladly say goodbye to each TT that you let go of, but always remember to watch for the next and the next and the next one to appear. Once you start this process, it will be a 24/7 engine running for the rest of your life.

When the Ten Commitments are memorized and become a mantra working for you 24/7, they will help you let go of your TT and free you from the devastating damage they cause. ♠

I am too lazy to let go and relax.

I know. You would have to stop everything you are not doing.

PLAY WINNING NO-LIMIT HOLD'EM AND LIFE

Less ego, less expectations, less demands, less lies, less resentments, less jealousy and less 'BS' means MORE MONEY.

BEING PRESENT is the ultimate blessing in poker and life. Just get rid of those distractions that keep you from being who you really are. If you are not who you really are, you are no one and nowhere. Call Mapquest for driving directions. Without your current location, they cannot help you.

To me, PRESENT is the most intriguing word in the English language. Think about it. Do you love to receive a *present*? Can you participate in any activity without being *present*? Where are you if you are not *present*? Why do you love to be with a person who is *present*? Wouldn't you say that Michael Jordan and Tiger Woods are beautiful to watch because they play their sport with the mastery of being *present* in the moment?

Let's get back to poker and explore the exercises we can do to put ourselves in the most optimal and effective *presence* at the poker table.

*Imagine the thrill of
being introduced to the Real
You and finding that you're A-OK...*

♦ Do not TRY to do or be anything. This may seem the opposite of all that you have learned or believed up to now. TRYING, in my experience, is not only ineffective, but gets in the way. It is another of those distractions we want to let go of.

♦ Our belief in our natural forces (like those that regulate our breathing and blood pressure) and our intention to notice and let go of TT are all we need to free us from them.

♦ Distractions are thoughts that cause fear, doubts, resentments, jealousies, expectations or any other thought that can block out our ability to make an unbiased choice.

♦ We are not attached to anything but a ship whose course we may choose.

♦ The more open and available (present) we are to the data coming in, the freer we are to consider the most choices possible and the more successful we will be.

♦ Consider the leader of the wolf pack. His presence is felt by the other wolves – just as the other players at the poker table feel the dominance of one player. His presence is an unsaid yet a profound force felt by all. Any player who can project that dominance gains a huge edge at the poker table.

The Thought Terrorists Within

Are you real or are you Memorex? Wouldn't it be wonderful to know and live the Real You? You can't get anywhere from nowhere, so accept it. After all, some force made you what and who you are. Only you are responsible for having taken a road to depart from who you really are. Wouldn't you agree a rose is a rose and knows it is not a daffodil? What would you have to give up? Simply all of your false ideas and beliefs about who you think you are and what you have made yourself into, and who you think you should be.

I have thought about this for many years. When I was in college, I would answer the question, "What's bothering you, Charlie?" with, "I'm more of what I am not than who I am." I finally understand that answer, after spending my entire life spinning my wheels in any direction other than becoming who I really am.

Becoming less of what I am not on a moment-to-moment basis feels like hitting the lottery because it liberates me. Each distraction – Thought Terrorist – contributes to what I am not.

As I notice any distraction (TT), I hold the INTENTION of letting go of it and my natural constructive forces free me from those ideas and thoughts about myself and others that have limited my vision of the world and all the possibilities that are presented to me each moment. They may appear destructive or constructive but should never be judged, just relinquished. In poker, blaming the dealer, bad luck or any idea you have about yourself – good or bad – are all examples of distractions.

Do not become attached to any idea or concept because you then become a prisoner of your belief system. Each moment is new and to be perceived as a clean slate. You will always be able to make your best choice in poker or in your life. Your instincts will start to work for you because you are not cluttered with old, useless and hurtful memories of past experiences anymore.

Remember: You do not need to do anything except notice each distraction the moment it appears. Hold the intention to let it go and trust and believe in yourself. You are who and what you are and you cannot change that. So embrace yourself and enjoy all that your life can be now. Imagine the thrill of being introduced to the Real You and finding that you're A-OK after all because you are truly who you really are. You take 100% responsibility. You are calm, confident, clear and you can focus as never before. Not a bad result.

When you make a decision at the poker table, you know it will be your best choice each time. You may be delighted with the opportunities to improve your chip position that may appear on a silver platter you have never dreamed of before. Win or lose, you know you have done your best.

You can now begin to play winning No-Limit Hold'em poker or you can embark on any journey your heart desires.

YOU ARE RICH! ♠

About the Article

In January and March, 2004, I wrote several articles that appeared in **Poker Player Newspaper.** *The response was so overwhelming (see "Thanks, Charlie"), that I expanded that information into this book.*

THE ARTICLE presents the concepts of Being Present (in the moment) and Being Who You Really Are and expands these concepts into the importance of being able to maintain FOCUS throughout an entire Poker tournament or any endeavor you may engage in. When discussing it with me, so many said, "Yes, Charlie, I agree, I'd love to 'Be More Present and Be Who I Really Am' but it's HARD TO DO."

This point is critical. Don't continue until you get it. If you are harboring the thought HARD TO DO, you probably believe it is a fact. This thought is based on your life's experience of being stuck in the knowledge that you would love to be more present and who you really are – but no matter how hard you've TRIED, you've made little or no progress.

You have convinced me. I will TRY to follow your advice.

@#$%^&*! Thank you. You have brought up a treasure trove of Thought Terrorists for me to let go of.

How many of you have just spotted in those remarks the two Thought Terrorists: HARD TO DO and TRYING? You have been harboring these all your life and you take them for granted. You believe them unquestionably and you probably have never even noticed them until I brought them up.

You certainly have never considered the terrible destruction that they do to your life, and you have never even considered the possibility of LETTING GO OF THEM. Let me explain: If you are TRYING, you can never succeed because TRYING to do something is making an effort to do something you don't know how to do. DOING something is accomplishing something. No one is perfect so all efforts are simply WHAT YOU ARE DOING. You are concerned about outcome if you are TRYING.

I TRY very hard to be brave, but change is too scary for me. I don't want to go there.

Do you realize what you have just said? You've chosen death over life!

"I don't know if I can or if my efforts will be good enough" are the thoughts behind the Thought Terrorist called TRYING. Can you imagine what your life might be if HARD TO DO and TRYING were banished from your mindset? The first step – and 95% of the job – is to NOTICE these two thoughts and to understand what is at stake.

Letting go of TRYING and HARD TO DO brings you into a world where all of your deepest hopes and dreams can come true. All of your future actions (without those two Thought Terrorists) can be DOING. Because you are not attached to the outcome anymore, you will be happy and at peace with your efforts and will embrace and find a prize in any outcome.

> Kindness, nobler ever than revenge.
>
> **WILLIAM SHAKESPEARE**

> Revenge smells sweet so it can destroy you. Kindness needs no such smell.
>
> **CHARLIE SHOTEN**

These are very simple points to grasp and even though obvious when pointed out, they are so subtle that few of us ever notice them, consider their effect or the

If I stop TRYING, will I ever accomplish anything?

Yes, you will have defeated the most dangerous TT – TRYING.

possibility of freeing ourselves from them. Now let's consider HARD TO DO and TRYING and apply my Ten Commitments to them.

Within a short period of time, HARD TO DO and TRYING will be greatly diminished and eventually eliminated from your mindset. Your ability to notice them and understand the terrible damage they do – from lost opportunities and clouded decision-making to stress and damage to your immune system – will alert you, and when you are no longer willing to put up with them, you will let go of them.

See your world with new eyes — eyes that will bring you that radiant smile I talk about so much and that will release your creativity and fulfill your deepest hopes and dreams for yourself and your loved ones.

My Ten Commitments are working for me 24/7 now with very little effort. They help me notice any Thought Terrorists I harbor, and then help me let go of them. I have no mercy for them. I do not negotiate with them. I do not give them an inch. It is either them or me and the rest of humanity. Can you imagine how good you will feel when your Terrorist Thoughts are gone from your mindset? You can do it. Rely on your intentions; trust and believe in yourself. Amen!

> Some think it's holding on that makes one strong.
>
> **SYLVIA ROBINSON**

> We now know it is Letting Go.
>
> **CHARLIE SHOTEN**

*Letting go of TRYING and HARD TO DO
brings you into a world where all
of your deepest hopes and
dreams can come true.*

Let's Cut to the Chase

We all can agree that it is desirable to:

If I have
new eyes,
what do I do
with the old
ones?

Give them
to your
worst TT
on its
way out.

♠ Be who we really are

♠ Be present in each new moment with a clean slate

♠ Focus throughout an entire poker tournament
or in any other endeavor

♠ Be calm and clear

♠ Wait for our best choice to appear

♠ Have a joyous mindset

♠ Learn from our experiences and not repeat our mistakes

♠ Put our ego aside and not let it sabotage our game and our lives

♠ Trust and believe in ourselves and to allow our instincts to guide us.

If I TRY to fail
and succeed,
which one
have I done?

You've
succeeded...
not deleted.

I could go on and on and make the case for all of the important mindsets of the really great poker pros (and all of the happy people in the world as well).

Self-help books sell the benefits of these wonderful traits. They give us years of information to acquire, hundreds of tools to buy to help us to get where we now know we all want to go, plenty of enthusiasm and positive thinking. Then they encourage and convince us that we can do it. We are left with a very constructive vision and we feel motivated to move forward to acquire all of these traits and to live by them. This is a very good thing. If I cast doubts on it, I risk arguing with the whole world; so let me share my thoughts.

> This above all:
> to thy own self be true.
>
> **WILLIAM SHAKESPEARE**

> Let go of the TT
> Self-deception.
>
> **CHARLIE SHOTEN**

You bought my book and have read it up to this point. I do not have any ideology to sell. I simply wish to point out that the most important thing left out of self-help books is a very simple HOW TO. While we are working feverishly to be all of the things we now know we want to be, we are being diverted from our real course of action which is to BE LESS OF WHAT WE ARE *NOT*. I am talking about the simple act of LETTING GO.

Before we can build, we need a clean foundation. This is true for any structure. A sculptor starts with a block of marble and removes the parts that conceal a Venus De Milo. The Venus was already there – inside that block of marble waiting to be set free!

All the great books on Earth promote being who you really are and living in the present. You have nothing new to offer.

A simple HOW TO is what I have to offer. That is new.

The greatest news is that we are already all that we are or could ever hope to be. We just need to let go of the alien parts (Thought Terrorists) we are holding onto. We now know what they are and where they are hiding. And we wait for them to appear so we can let go of them one by one.

Now the Big Finish

So now I will share my Roadmap of instructions – my Ten Commitments – to show you how to identify and let go of the TT you have been harboring and nurturing far too long. I do not have hundreds of tools to sell, nor ask that you spend large amounts of money and time supporting me. I just suggest you review my book as many times as you need to, and put into motion my suggestions. They are simple to understand and easy to do. You have little to lose and a whole new life to gain. ♠

How can you possibly say that all my problems will be solved and I can relax and enjoy my life at the same time? Everyone knows that hard work is necessary for any worthwhile venture.

Hard work is fun, if HARD TO DO is not your mindset.

*The greatest news
is that we are already
all that we are or
could ever hope to be.*

Thought Terrorists	Feelings Caused by TT
Hard to Do	Resentment
Trying	Resignation
Ego	Jealousy
Expectations	Contempt
Hurtful Memories	Grudges
Superiority	Hate
Inferiority	Vindictiveness
Doubt	Irrational Fears
Faults	Anxiety
Poor Self-image	Depression
Self-destruction	Stress
Arrogance	Anger
Greed	Revenge
Victimization	Hurt
Impatience	Self-pity
	Compulsions
	Addictions

Desirable Mindsets

Clean / Delete / Let Go

Focus - Focus - Focus

Embrace Every Outcome

Present

Happy

Joyous

Patient

No Attachment to Outcome

Self Acceptance

Calm, Confident and Clear

Love - Love - Love

Believe in Yourself

Identify Distractions / Let Go Of

Less Fear / Courage

Be Yourself

Attitude is Gratitude

Trust Yourself

Intention

Healthy Mind / Body

Ten Commitments 24/7

Notice TT
Notice TT
Notice TT
Let go of
Let go of
Let go of
Be less of what you are not
Be less of what you are not
Be less of what you are not
Be who you really are
Be who you really are
Be who you really are
A joyous mindset
A joyous mindset
A joyous mindset
A radiant contagious smile
A radiant contagious smile
A radiant contagious smile

WHAAAT?

My Ten Commitments

1 MY ATTITUDE IS GRATITUDE

Imagine the thousands of situations that would make your current
concerns seem minor. Get the point?
Accept yourself and your current situation. It is what it is.
Your old perception is what upsets you.
Replace that old perception with your new one.

2 I FOCUS ON MY INNER SELF AND LOOK AFTER AND CARE FOR IT.

Embrace and trust who you really are 24/7.
If you don't, no one will.

3 I NOTICE EVERY MEMORY, THOUGHT, IDEA OR BELIEF THAT I AM HOLDING THAT INFLICTS STRESS.

You cannot let go of a Thought Terrorist until you find it.
When you notice TT, you are 95% home.
Now you can let go of it. You give it power by holding onto it.
Take away its power and you can let go of it.

4 **I HOLD MY INTENTIONS TO LET GO OF TT AND FREE MYSELF FROM HOLDING ONTO THEM AS I REGISTER THE FULL MEASURE OF THE HARM THEY ARE INFLICTING UPON ME.**

Intentions are powerful. They can move mountains.

Never underestimate the power of your intentions.

Why would you give power or control over your life to a terrorist?

Your intentions, without any other effort by you, will do the job.

Focusing your intentions to let go of TT leaves no room for them to exist.

Unconditional love and prayer are part of your intentions.

5 **I BELIEVE AND TRUST IN MYSELF. I FREE MYSELF FROM HOLDING ONTO TT BY LETTING GO OF THEM.**

What choice do you have? Own your own power and use it.

Like most of us, you may have sold yourself short.

You have free will.

No outside force can make you do anything unless you let it.

Become a warrior for your own interests.

You can do no more good for yourself and those you love.

6

I AM CALM, CONFIDENT AND CLEAR AND I WAIT FOR MY BEST CHOICE TO APPEAR AFTER CONSIDERING ALL OF MY CHOICES AND THE CONSEQUENCES OF EACH. WHEN MY BEST CHOICE APPEARS, I ACT.

Wait for your turn to act.

Consider your many choices and their consequences.

When your best choice in poker or in life appears, act on it.

Trust that it will appear and that you will know it when it does.

It may take time, but soon it will appear like clockwork.

7

I AM NOT ATTACHED TO OUTCOME – I LOOK FOR THE BENEFIT, AND WELCOME AND EMBRACE ANY AND EVERY OUTCOME THAT APPEARS.

Always be surprised and welcome each outcome with open arms
and curiosity.

Don't judge the result.

You will receive wonderful benefits previously hidden from your view.

Experience plays this role in your evolution.

8   I FORGIVE AND ASK FOR FORGIVENESS.

I humbly ask for forgiveness from all those whom I have knowingly or unknowingly neglected or abused (by TT) through words, thoughts and deeds and humbly grant forgiveness to those who knowingly or unknowingly have neglected or abused me (by TT) through their words, thoughts and deeds.

9   I NOTICE THE NEXT THOUGHT TERRORIST (AND THE NEXT AND THE NEXT) AS IT APPEARS AND REPEAT COMMITMENTS #3 THROUGH #8.

Once again, focus on any harmful feelings and thoughts.
Notice the thoughts that cause them.
Measure the harm they are inflicting.
Repeat Commitments #3 through #8.

10   I MAINTAIN MY ATTITUDE OF GRATITUDE.

The first thought always in my conscious mind is "My attitude is gratitude."
My last thought of the day is to give thanks for my attitude of gratitude. ♠

Feelings

WE HAVE TALKED about harmful thoughts, ideas, beliefs and memories that create feelings like stress. I hope you can now see their devastation to our physical being and how they cause anxiety and can cut off our deepest hopes and aspirations. You may also see how we not only put up with them, but also harbor and nurture them. Holding onto them is an unconscious and automatic reflex of which we are unaware.

> Self-love my liege, is not so vile a sin as self-neglecting.
>
> **WILLIAM SHAKESPEARE**

> Treat yourself kindly
> Look after yourself and care for yourself.
>
> **CHARLIE SHOTEN
> (2nd Commitment)**

These foreign invaders are as real as the masked terrorists holding innocent civilians until they behead them. Our TT also kill us, but more slowly. The debilitating stress they create damages our immune system, creates fear and all kinds of self-destructive behavior. They also prevent us from being who we really are and block out our creativity.

My brother-in-law's TT are awful. What should I advise my sister?

Wait until he stops beating her, then tie him up and drop him in the nearest river.

Love and fear are the prime motivators in our lives. We want to keep and enjoy love, but we need to get rid of the thoughts, ideas and beliefs that are our enemy. Our harmful feelings are actually our best scouts. When we feel fear, we can trace the thoughts creating it, and sure enough, we have TT in our sight.

Now we know what they are, how they are killing us and how to let go of them. We have no mercy for them. When we let go of them, they will never bother us again.

My daughter once loaned the car I was expecting to use during my visit with her to someone else. She knew I was coming and how much I needed it. When it was unavailable, I immediately experienced feelings of anger and resentment. What a gift!

 My dog is berserk with TT. Can you help him?

 Loosen his collar.

I traced the thoughts I was holding – all I had done for her, she doesn't care about me, etc. – used my Ten Commitments and focused my intention to let go of my terrorist thoughts. Two hours later, I was free from their effect on me. I could now have the relationship with my daughter that I wanted without resentment interfering. I also felt much better about myself, which was the relationship with myself I really wanted. The areas of my life that were affected by anger and resentment were forever gone.

> Doubts are traitors, and make us lose the good we oft might win, by fearing to attempt.
>
> **WILLIAM SHAKESPEARE**

> Have no compassion for your doubts. We now know the measure of harm they do to us.
>
> **CHARLIE SHOTEN**

Have you ever considered the role that fear plays in your life? Now you are equipped to do something about it. Freedom from irrational fear is a priceless gift. Though fear is necessary for basic survival, when caused by destructive thoughts, fear can limit and even ruin your life.

Okay, I will go for it. Now will you leave me alone?

Yes, I will, but only so you have something to be grateful for.

I have always yearned for those lost opportunities I never took advantage of. These are the greatest losses of all because the universe is continually offering unlimited gifts in unimaginable ways.

There are dimensions the caterpillar could never experience if it didn't transform into a butterfly. If you take the time to consider it, there is so much more than what we can see, feel or touch. If we are open to receive the many gifts laid out before us by a generous universe, we can use our discernment to choose what is right and perfect for each of us. ♦

> What is necessary to change a person is to change his awareness of himself.
> **ABRAHAM MASLOW**

> When he becomes aware of what he is holding onto that he is not, he can let go of it and be who he already is.
> **CHARLIE SHOTEN**

Should I have a going-away party every time I let go of a Thought Terrorist?

Only if you are sure it won't show up.

If you take the time to consider it, there is so much more than what we can see, feel or touch.

Memories

Your Presence at the Poker Table as a Metaphor for Any Area of Your Life

IF YOU ARE PREOCCUPIED with memories of past experiences or present concerns, you will miss valuable information at the poker table. If you are distracted by TT, you will miss the changing dynamics and won't know if someone is holding good cards or just bluffing.

On the other hand, if you are present in the moment and not distracted by TT, without effort you will find yourself with a stronger awareness of the other players and their actions. It's called INTUITION and you either get it or you don't. All good players consider the same poker issues in any hand. Your instincts can help you get an idea of the thoughts and strategies of any player you focus on.

> There is no good or bad but that our thinking makes it so.
>
> **WILLIAM SHAKESPEARE**

> Our thinking must stop judging everything. What is, is so.
>
> **CHARLIE SHOTEN**

If I am not who I believe myself to be, can you introduce me to who I really am?

I will find out when you are available, then give you a call and set up an appointment.

We are now back to the main topic of this book: HOW TO BE LESS OF WHAT YOU ARE NOT. The emotional scars caused by TT you are holding onto are in your way. Let's look at what we can do to start this process of letting go of TT and getting rid of those scars. Put my Ten Commitments into motion to become a 24/7 search engine for TT.

My Ten Commitments	
1	**Attitude**
2	**Focus**
3	**Notice**
4	**Intention**
5	**Trust**
6	**Appear**
7	**Outcome**
8	**Forgiveness**
9	**Notice**
10	**Gratitude**

Now that I can maintain my focus for days at a time, won't it be boring to have no distractions?

Certainly! No more balls up in the air to juggle all the time will let you spend more time with yourself.

It's simple. It's easy.

I'm doing it. So can you.

If your newly experienced freedom isn't a big enough reward, just enjoy your poker winnings. ♠

Self Esteem

"Until you free yourself to trust your own inner direction, your experience will be LIMITED by your beliefs. Once you are liberated to follow your own inner direction, your experience will SHAPE your beliefs."

Letter to Earth: *Who We Are Becoming... What We Need to Know*
by Elia Wise

B Y NOW, you have read my Article and much of my material. It makes sense, but you are holding a lifetime of experiences that have convinced you that most efforts to free yourself bring defeat and more trauma. Your self-esteem and self-image are too dear for you to rock the boat. You have come to terms with your life, particularly if you are successful and have money and status in our evolving society.

Consider the price that you and those closest to you pay for your resistance to change. Few of us look forward to change and most rarely will go there if not pushed. It is a lost opportunity to free yourself from the baggage you created and have held onto since your first traumatic experience of neglect and/or abuse. I call this baggage Thought Terrorists (TT). Until you let go of them, you will experience physical and mental deterioration at a much faster pace than you otherwise would. I am talking about every disease you will ever experience. We must change our efforts from mindlessly holding onto our TT to noticing

Sometimes I am happy, sometimes I am sad.

Sometimes you are who you are and sometimes you are who you are not!

and letting go of them. Failing to do this would be a lost opportunity to be less of what you are not so you can be who you really are.

Welcome to CONSCIOUSNESS. It is the all of the all that is. We are distracted and blinded by traumatic memories that keep us from experiencing our full potential. We are being held hostage by these memories, and ironically, we are their guards and wardens as well as their loyal supporters. We have been doing everything we can to support and comfort them, even as they are killing us with no mercy.

Can I rely on my intentions to work without effort as regularly as my breathing?

Only if you trust and believe in yourself.

Wake up and let go of the old to experience the new. The old sees change as a threat (which it is to TT) and fights with everything in its power to hold it off. Without change, there is no life, so register this and act as if your life depends on it because it does. The unseen, unknown and unfamiliar are limitless, and more than we can ever comprehend. Let's commit to embracing change every moment of every day. No more friction, no more stress...just peace. The chance and hope of being who I really am in the present moment turns me on more than any prize or fortune I could ever imagine. I am going for it. How about you?

> Keeping score of old scores and scars, getting even and one-upping is your worst enemy.
>
> **MALCOLM FORBES**

> Become a Thought Terrorist Hunter and you will really settle old scores.
>
> **CHARLIE SHOTEN**

You believe so many things about yourself – your taste in music and art, your skill in poker, business, sports, etc. Do these beliefs define who you are?

Does reconsidering them threaten your ego and self-esteem? Self-esteem can be a false security blanket limiting your chances for a more creative, enjoyable and fulfilled life. Your concept of what and who you are may not be supporting you. You are fully supported when you are truly who you are, without relying on any medals, titles, awards, achievements, concepts or beliefs.

If I can maintain
my focus,
will I become
rich?

No, you
will already
be rich.

Break out of your self-imposed limitations. They are only there to keep you in your resigned state in life, to keep you safe (in your eyes) and hassle-free, while you give up the best hopes and dreams living deep within your being. Consider the risk and reward. You may feel you will not land on your feet, but you may be delighted to find out how strong and beautiful you really are. Give up your self-esteem support system. Gain a whole new life. How fragile are you? That is your main obstacle. ♠

What if I am
not a beautiful
person if I become
who I really am?

You can always
change your
perception of
the concept
"beautiful."

54

Embracing change is exemplified by the magnificent new Wynn Tower of 2005, rising from the site of the old Desert Inn Hotel built in 1950.

TT No More

I HAVE A VISION of each of us taking a stand and not putting up with our TT any more. I invite you to participate as an active and equal member.

This will be a very personal and selfish enterprise where our main focus is to notice our own TT when they show their ugly faces, see the damage they do to us and hold our intention to let go of them every minute of every day.

We can support each other by sharing our experiences. This will be like a treasure hunt in reverse. Instead of rushing out to find treasure, we will be calm, confident, clear and focused and we will wait patiently for our TT of the moment to appear. We will be thankful and as excited as if we hit the lottery when they appear so we can let go of them. And we will share our moment of self-discovery of who we really are with each other. Can you imagine anything that could be more fun or constructive?

> When you reach for the stars, you may not quite get one, but you won't come up with a handful of mud either.
>
> **LEO BURNETT**

Once our Ten Commitments are in motion, they will continue to work as regularly as our breathing.

No more TRYING or HARD TO DO. All our efforts will come from a place deep within and will reflect our passionate desires.

Now let's get down to the practical ways that we can all participate in TT HUNTS.

I've had enough! No more crazy ideas or I will give your book back to you and demand a refund.

You really know how to hurt a Guru.

Ways We Can Participate

- ♠ Breakfast Meetings
- ♠ Website: www.nolimitlife.net
- ♠ E-mail (spread the word/share)
- ♠ Seminars/Workshops
- ♠ Classes at Corporations
- ♠ Distribution in Prisons
- ♠ Classes at Schools/Universities
- ♠ Television Productions
- ♠ Movie Productions (perhaps an animated film about Thought Terrorists and how children can recognize them)
- ♠ Television Talk Show, featuring poker tournaments with insightful commentary about TT as appropriate, in addition to strategies involved in poker play
- ♠ Educational television program sharing the poker experience
- ♠ Series of CDs/DVDs
- ♠ Follow-up book of how readers' lives have been affected

I have a wonderful life, beautiful family, plenty of money and a great golf game. Can you help me?

My advice, young man, is NOT to read my book. You might find dangerous insights.

Letting Go of Thought Terrorists

M Y TEN COMMITMENTS are the engine that helps me let go of my Thought Terrorists (TT). Now I am always on the lookout for them.

With each TT that I notice and let go of, I free myself that much more to allow my instincts to help guide me in whatever pursuit is right and perfect in the current moment. That pursuit is good, can never be predicted and is always a beautiful surprise. I would not have it any other way.

One by one, I let go of each thought, memory, idea or belief I hold that causes me stress or does not serve my best interests. I methodically follow my Roadmap to let go of them until they are all gone. With fewer shackles to limit my reach, each day is new and beautiful with wonderful exciting possibilities. I will rarely be bored again. Only when I was burdened and bound in the confines of those ancient hurtful memories, thoughts, beliefs and ideas was I bored, depressed and overwhelmed with anxieties.

I now keep an open mind about myself, others and life. I don't DRIVE myself to excel, accumulate, buttress my self-esteem and worth, or look to another to fill me up and make me whole. I expose all of my TT to my Ten Commitments and let them help me do the job that needs to be done. What a burden is lifted. I can relax, be confident and know that I will fulfill all of my healthy hopes, dreams and aspirations. This is surely one of the "heavens on earth" everyone talks about.

How can I diminish my TT?

Join our TT HUNTERS GROUP 24/7.

I am totally motivated 24/7 to let my pure instincts and inspirations help guide me. Carrying less TT baggage that creates fear, anxiety, despair, hopelessness, alienation, anger, confusion, frustration and so many other feelings that cause me physical and mental dis-ease is no longer a burden. This is a fairly new process for me. In the past, it never occurred to me to let go of the hurtful concepts about myself that I was holding onto. Now I focus on any TT baggage I can identify and use my Ten Commitments to free myself by letting go of them.

> Life is like an ever-shifting kaleidoscope – a slight change and all patterns alter.
>
> **SHARON SALTZBERG**

> Shift your focus from SEEKING to FINDING. Instead of TRYING HARDER, LET GO OF.
>
> **CHARLIE SHOTEN**

These Commitments, which I memorized, are a friendly chant in my mind at all times. They are my solid ground and leave no room for TT to do their dirty deeds. Each TT that I notice, I let go of. I maintain my focus throughout each poker tournament (or any endeavor), and as I focus on what I am not and let go of each TT, my ability to focus is enhanced. This process grows more powerful every day. Who said that growing older is not a blessing? I have a joyous mindset and a radiant contagious smile because of my new-found freedom. How can I not help but smile when I look forward to this whole new Charlie each and every morning!

What are the qualifications to become a member of your TT HUNTERS GROUP?

Your birth certificate and Bar Mitzvah pictures.

Surrender in a Crisis

When I was sixteen years old, I went on a skiing trip to Mount Snow in Vermont. Upon reaching the lodge, I was asked which slope I wished to ski. I had been an avid ice skater and had even entered the speed skating trials for the Silver Skates at Central Park in New York City. Because I had no concept of limits at that time, I was vehement to ski only the steepest and most advanced slope. After all, I could skate with abandon and didn't think about the different skills that skiing required. I had never had a lesson, never put on a pair of skis or didn't even know how to snow plow to slow down.

> Lord! We know what we are, but know not what we may be.
>
> **WILLIAM SHAKESPEARE**

> The beauty of life begins where the unseen meets the unknown.
>
> **CHARLIE SHOTEN**

I remember skiing downhill and concentrating on keeping my balance. Within a short time, I was speeding down the slope faster and faster and totally out of control. I knew in a split second that I was going to crash into the trees in front of me. I had no idea of my speed at that moment, but it could have been over 50 mph. I knew that I might be hurt, even killed, and when that thought came into my mind, I thought, "If I go totally limp, my bones won't break."

Make me a winner.

You are a winner. Certificate and ribbon – $250 please.

I had never been told that by anyone and it was a pure survival reflex. That is the action I took, going completely limp and surrendering to whatever the outcome would be. I wound up embedded in the snow and could not move. When rescued, I walked away without a scratch.

In a crisis or any of life's endeavors, letting go, surrendering, stopping all efforts or just going limp is an alternative to TRYING to figure out what to do or to continuing the stressful activities in which you are engaged in an effort to free yourself.

When we do this, an interesting process occurs. We release our attachments to the visions we have about the current crisis, and free ourselves to a potential shift in perception where alternate solutions and outcomes can emerge. ♣

I know I can ski because I have skied since I was a kid. How can I be sure that I will survive if I surrender the beliefs I rely on to assure me that I am okay?

A part of you that you wish to survive may be the baggage you are carrying that is hurting and limiting you. How can you surrender if you continue to hold on so tightly and sustain these enemies when you recognize who they really are and the terrible destruction they may be causing in your life? See the enemy.

Man's Inhumanity to Man

LOOK BACK IN HISTORY at man's inhumanity to man throughout the ages. Anyone slightly aware of the carnage in the 20th century knows how much destruction has taken place. We can look at it macro – World War II, for instance; or we can look at it micro – the painful experiences that separate us from our closest family and loved ones.

We can either choose to wake up and let go of our Thought Terrorists (TT) now and free ourselves to be all of what we already are, or we can do nothing about them and continue to suffer the consequences. If we can't do this for ourselves, we must do it for our children.

From birth we are led away, mentally and physically, from our true knowing selves. We are taught, motivated, scolded, intimidated and brainwashed – you name it – onto paths designed to keep us in line, to help us survive, to make us better, to conform to the culture, to bolster our self-esteem and to teach us right from wrong and every other way that can be devised to force us into a vision that we most likely do not and would not share unless it were shoved down our throat. It is implanted like a computer virus by well-meaning elders who are controlled by their own Thought Terrorists.

I have studied human history all of my life. We are always killing ourselves and each other. What is the point? Why bother?

I see your point. Do you prefer the gun or the sword?

We are born with the innate knowledge of integral values that connect us. It is our heritage and comes with being human. We need no verbal teaching of integral values – only the demonstration of them by our parents and caretakers. All efforts to force us to stay in line only serve to separate, not connect us.

Memorize my Ten Commitments and make them a 24/7 mindset as a firewall and thrasher of any and all TT you are harboring. Soon your new joyous mindset will do its job as regularly as your breathing and with the same lack of effort.

If man's inhumanity to man causes the litigation that is destroying our health care system, whose Thought Terrorists are responsible?

I can't expose the ACLU. They will get a cease-and-desist order of my book.

This may not be clear to you yet, but if you think about it and put it into practice, you will grasp it. Hopefully, you will then suffer less from bad beats in poker and in life. Your joyous mindset will cause you to have that radiant contagious smile I warned you about on the front cover. ♣

Intentions

INTENTIONS are a strong force in the creation process. Do all living things hold intentions? Birds migrate, salmon swim upstream to procreate and trees adjust to climate conditions. Do they also hold intentions? If so, are human intentions different from all other forms of life?

"As you ask, so shall you receive" is a quote that many of us know and believe. Perhaps this is the difference between us and other life forms. We can also ask for our deepest dreams to come true, even pray for them. Many of us can attest to the power of prayer. Much has been spoken and written about it. In times of crisis, ASKING and PRAYER offer a special focus with enormous power behind it to comfort and assist us in getting through the hardest of times.

I hate so many people and so many things. Is hating such a bad thing?

Only for the one who hates.

Perhaps including ASKING and PRAYER in our meaning of intentions can add to its power to help us let go of the destructive memories, ideas, thoughts and beliefs we are holding that are killing us. Let's add UNCONDITIONAL LOVE into this process to energize and power our intentions to help free us once and for all. If we do nothing about our TT and continue to host them, we risk our lives, and dis-ease will surely follow the stress that is created by them.

Even though we are not aware that we harbor and nurture our TT as valued guests, why tolerate their devastation to our well-being as passive victims. We can do something about them.

Let's add UNCONDITIONAL LOVE
into this process to energize
and power our intentions to
help free us once and for all.

It never occurred to me that the TT are controlling me.

It never occurred to you that you could do something about them either.

Consider the scenario of hostages being held by terrorists. The hostages are tied up and blindfolded, each dreading the moment he or she may be beheaded. In that circumstance, who wouldn't pray for their freedom? This danger is similar to the one presented by TT. Here, your prayers for freedom from danger would be part of your intentions as stated in my Fourth Commitment. If we do fail to hold these intentions and do nothing about our TT, the stress they cause will expose us to dis-ease.

We will also expose our children to all of the destructive consequences of our own TT. We can make prayer and unconditional love a part of our intentions to empower us to let go of our greatest enemy – our TT – and to be less of what we are NOT and to be who we really are, have a joyous mindset and a radiant contagious smile. We must urgently follow this process to achieve happiness and peace and to free ourselves from the chains imprisoning us.

We spend our time worrying about all kinds of possible scenarios that might be visited upon us from outside circumstances. Let's change our focus to the internal forces that are the real threats to our lives – the parasitic thoughts we unknowingly host as invited and treasured guests that on a 24/7 basis are doing their deadly deeds to us. ◆

> (He is) very proud, revengeful, ambitious, with more offenses at (his) beck than (he) has thoughts to put them in, imagination to give them shape, or time to act them in.
>
> **WILLIAM SHAKESPEARE**

> Let's pray for him, and also pray for him to leave us alone.
>
> **CHARLIE SHOTEN**

We spend our time worrying
about all kinds of possible
scenarios that might be
visited upon us from
outside circumstances.

New Outlook

As my book evolved and came into being, a new outlook emerged.

♣ Life instead of Death

♣ Integrity instead of Dishonesty

♣ Joy instead of Gloom

♣ Giving instead of Receiving

♣ Democracy instead of Despotism

♣ Freedom instead of Slavery

 If I become less of what I am not, will I become more of who I am?

 No, you are already all of who you are. You will let go of your TT baggage.

William Shakespeare said it:

To Be or Not To Be. THAT is the question.

Charlie Shoten replies:

To Focus or Not To Focus

To Notice or Not To Notice

To Let Go Of or Not To Let Go Of

To Be Less of What You Are NOT or To Be More of What You Are NOT

To Have a Joyous Mindset or Not To Have a Joyous Mindset

To Have a Radiant Contagious Smile or Not To Have a Radiant Contagious Smile

To Practice the Ten Commitments or Not To Practice the Ten Commitments

The TT baggage we carry imprisons and destroys us. We now know that our main focus is to notice this baggage, focus our intentions on it within our Ten Commitments and let go of it to free ourselves from it.

This is an evolutionary shift away from TRYING and HARD TO DO. We can now embrace not only the ecstasy and the glory of our successful results, but also the disappointment and pain of our failures as an opportunity to grow.

The pain, the glory, the ecstasy and all of the dreaded results we fear will become our outcome are replaced by a simple embrace of them. We now know to view all presents offered to us and discover within them their message and benefits without rejection because they are not what we seek. All of our results, whether successful or not, are gifts offering benefits we would never have perceived before.

Yes, we can even embrace death along with everything else that our journey in this world brings us. The alternative is the friction, stress and mental/physical harm that disharmony in life always brings. ◆

Becoming who I really am and living in the present sounds nice. What's the catch?

Your doubts and fears.

How I Prepare

WHEN A TEST was given during my school days, my thoughts were always scattered until I prepared a summary of each subject that was going to be on the test. A poker tournament is also a test. My Ten Commitments work the same way as the summaries I prepared for school tests. And I refer to them before, during and after each tournament, as well as all other activities in which I am involved.

> How poor are they who have not patience.
>
> **WILLIAM SHAKESPEARE**

> He who exercises discernment is a patient man.
>
> **CHARLIE SHOTEN**

Following my Ten Commitments, my intention is to be calm, confident and clear so I can focus during the long hours required to win any tournament. A tournament is not a 100-yard dash. I need all my strength to maintain focus throughout, especially at the final table; so I rest as much as possible during the tournament whenever I can safely take my eyes off the current action. One distraction or compulsive act can send me out the door. Plus it's important to project a confident image and a dominant presence.

How can I ever hope to become a great poker player?

You can start by noticing the ideas you hold onto about yourself, other poker players, and beliefs that you take for granted, but do not serve you.

My Ten Commitments are always at the forefront of my mind, ready to handle every Thought Terrorist. They help me let go of them so I am not distracted from the action at the table. As soon as my mind raises the question, "Will I know what to do when it's my turn to act?" or any other fear or doubt enters my head, I automatically think:

It's important to project a confident image and a dominant presence.

Attitude

Focus

Notice

Intentions

Trust

Appear

Outcome

Forgiveness

Notice

Gratitude

My Thought Terrorists are loyal to me. They keep assuring me that I am God. How can I kill them?

With my TEN COMMITMENTS.

Not only do my Commitments help me let go of doubts, but also any other TT that interfere with my decision-making process. Holding my Commitments at the forefront of my mind leaves no room for TT to exist and hurt me. Holding my intentions to let go of them give them little chance to harm my game and my life. They have become my ten guardians for the rest of my life. By repeating them over and over, I have implanted them in my mindset where they help me let go of TT 24/7.

This is my formula for mental preparation. It takes time and discipline for it all to come together. Call it my security blanket, crutch or anything else, but it is the tool that works for me – the one I rely on in all my life's activities.

We all recognize the most successful poker players on the tour. They are usually smiling, helpful, at peace with themselves and quietly confident. As soon as my ego projects thoughts that affect my actions at a tournament, I don't go very far. One-upsmanship and getting even with someone always hurts me. This happened recently and I had to apologize to Hason Habib, whom I offended. I left the tournament in 13th place, knowing that my own ego had beaten me.

Why is everyone so happy to see me when I enter the poker room?

They need to pay the rent or buy a new car.

> (These are) diseas'd ventures that play with all infirmities for gold.
>
> **WILLIAM SHAKESPEARE**

> While playing with infirmities for gold, missing out on all the fun?
>
> **CHARLIE SHOTEN**

My Ten Commitments are the most constructive thing I focus on. It is best to be a clear vessel with no preconceived thoughts or ideas to interfere with your decision-making process. Hopefully, you will have allowed your mind to take in all of the visual and vocal energy at the table so your instincts can help you make your best decision after you have considered your choices and their consequences.

We all have walked down this dark alley many times before. We have sensed those players holding big hidden hands (sets) that can do us in. I am particularly alert in those situations where I must uncover the size and nature of the potential ambush by any unknown hand in a tournament. I also need to discover the information that will assist me in making the best choice.

I've gotten used to stress and depression. I won't know myself.

It is a big risk. Your life may be very different.

To do this, I must pressure my opponent in every possible way to reveal the relative strength of his hand. This includes my demeanor as well as my chosen action. My action is based on my stack size as well as his, my current position in the tournament, the payout scales, the current and future size of the blinds and many other factors.

I always consider in advance what my action will be if my opponent makes various responses. If I take my time to consider my choices and their consequences and let my instincts guide me, I will be confident that I have done my best job.

My belief and trust in myself will let my vast experience and instincts help me make my best choice. Acting compulsively or because I am tired or just want to gamble is not what I want to do. I have been there and done that enough times. I want to make my best choice and play each hand correctly.

When I do, winning takes care of itself in the long run. ♣

My mind can overcome anything. I've read *Think and Grow Rich* over 100 times

I will leave you $5 today so you can eat dinner.

All of our results, whether successful or not,
are gifts offering benefits we would
never have perceived before.

At the Poker Table

WHEN CARDS ARE DEALT to me, I welcome them and remember them. I am neither disappointed nor ecstatic about them. Any two cards represent an opportunity and a danger. If I am always looking for Aces, I will be disappointed most of the time. I look to use any two cards to improve my chip position or to lose as little as possible. I welcome all cards I am dealt.

Let go of your preconceived ideas and be a clear vessel. Your instincts must be the biggest part and foundation of your decision-making process. You have played countless hands where your instincts have all this information available to them. By now, even the math involved in any hand is sensed way before your thinking does the exact calculations.

Hopefully, my Sixth Commitment alerts you to take your time and wait for your best choice to appear after considering all your choices and their consequences. Then you can act with precision and the confidence that comes from knowing that you have made your best choice. This will help you project a dominant force at the table. The other players will respect and fear you. What could give you a bigger advantage?

I am not delving deep into the math and specific poker strategy in this book. There are already so many good books and DVDs available on that subject. Instead I am addressing the mindset and self-mastery necessary to excel at poker. It is the most important part of poker and the most difficult to master with the least amount of information available. ◆

> Their hats are plucked about their ears, and half their faces buried in their cloaks.
>
> **WILLIAM SHAKESPEARE**

> And some with dark glasses in an attempt to hide their fear, motives and expressions fool only themselves at the poker table.
>
> **CHARLIE SHOTEN**

Welcome all cards you are dealt.

Mindsets

MY SIXTH COMMITMENT is always repeating itself in my mindset when I sit down in any tournament. I am calm, confident and clear. I wait for my best choice to appear after considering all of my choices and the consequences of each. It is a mantra that helps me focus, be patient and stay alert to all that is going on at my table. As soon as my ego, any doubts or distracting thoughts (TT) appear, my Sixth Commitment takes front and center in my mindset and allows me to concentrate on the action at the table.

When the cards are dealt, I know I will make the best choice when it is my turn to act. I always consider my gut feelings and allow my instincts to guide me. The actions of the players before me and the possible actions of the players after me are considered, as are the risks and reward of any choices I am considering: the amount of the blinds, the size of each player's stack and all other relevant information at the table. There is always an upside and a downside in every hand.

Remember:

◆ Whenever possible, be active and aggressive in every stage of a tournament.

◆ Even when you run card-dead, always consider stealing the blinds.

◆ Make strategic bets with weak hands.

◆ If you are not active and willing to gamble with a weak hand, few or no players will gamble with you when you bet a strong one.

- Be confident in your game and trust your decisions or realize that you are paying your dues for now, until you can achieve the presence and acquire the skills you need.

- Every tournament offers you a wealth of knowledge.

- Study all of the players, particularly the successful ones.

- See if you can understand their thinking processes and their strategies. Look for the clues that are all over the table and don't be afraid to act on them.

- There is no substitute for EXPERIENCE.

Mindsets of the Great Pros

Let Go of All Distractions	Be Willing to Fold Any Hand
Be Confident	Consider Other Players' Mindsets
Be Focused	Be Joyous
Stay Alert	Be Optimistic
Be Patient	Act Decisively
Be All Business	Learn from Experience
Be Willing to Risk	Have an Exit Strategy
Protect All Your Chips	Be Courteous
Consider All Information	Maintain Integrity

No-Limit Strategies

Short Stack

I have had a lot of success playing late in tournaments with a short stack. I once won a tournament when I was down to one chip. In another, I came in Second when I was down to $1300 in chips at the final table with $500,000 in play.

Both times I was tenacious, never gave up nor got steamed after a bad beat and never doubted my belief that I was going to win. I did not panic and I calmly waited for the right time and the right hand. I never let myself think that I am not gambling in any poker hand – or in life, for that matter. There is always an element of risk. One of the biggest errors I see players make is not being willing to stick their necks out and risk it all when that is precisely what is called for. I can look back at so many times when I have made that tough call or even the tougher desperate raise.

> I will most humbly take my leave of you. You cannot, sir, take from me anything that I will not more willingly part with.
>
> **WILLIAM SHAKESPEARE**

> Sometimes the parasite shows intentions to eat his host and starves himself.
>
> **CHARLIE SHOTEN**

How can I tell if someone is bluffing?

See if you have the NUTS and if so, raise him.

I saw Mark Seif raise all in at a critical time in a recent tournament and he quadrupled up, became the chip leader and won. Later that day, he hinted to me he was only on a draw. Recently I asked him again about that hand and this time he told me the truth: he had flopped top set. I thought he was bluffing. He was not. Either way, he would have won!

I keep getting bad beats in every tournament. Any suggestions?

Let me know what tournament table you are on. I will help you out.

Whether early or late in a tournament, you need to accumulate chips, not just to survive, but also to have a chance to reach the final table and win First Place. It is easier to win chips early on because most of your opponents are inexperienced players and many are playing tight scared poker. Gamble with players you can read.

Reading the relative strength of another's hand is your biggest advantage. Enter pots to see the flop (considering the risk and reward) and then outplay your opponents. That is another reason to call or raise often early in the tournament. You won't necessarily need to flop the best hand to win the pot.

Image

Should I sit up straight or lean one way or the other at the poker table?

Definitely the other.

Your image at the table is always important. Project a dominance that intimidates. This doesn't require any particular action – just a confident presence. But you cannot fake it. It must be real. No one should ever be comfortable playing against you or able to put you on a hand. If you are considered predictable, you are at a big disadvantage, unless you turn it around like Dan Harrington does. In a discussion of his World Series play, he said he likes to project predictability to hide the fact that he is totally unpredictable.

If you are not willing to take risks in poker and in life, you might as well save your entry fee and not sign up to play or even get out of bed.

> Everything that grows holds in perfection but a little moment.
>
> **WILLIAM SHAKESPEARE**

Large Stack

Your stack in a tournament is never large enough if you do not have 100% of the chips in play. Focus on opportunities to increase your chip position and be diligent in protecting yourself from losing even one of them.

> We grow or we die. It's called living.
>
> **CHARLIE SHOTEN**

When I was at the final table at the Borgata Open, everyone thought I was letting the other players eliminate one another because I rarely played a hand. As it turned out, everyone did eliminate each other until I found myself head-up. The truth is I ran card-dead for many hours and I just looked smart. I was deeply concerned that I couldn't find a hand to get my chips into the pot. I went from $450,000 down to $125,000 and then found myself head-up with Nolie Franciosa who had over $2.5 million in chips. Second Place is a good result but not where I wanted to be. I got back up to $800,000 in chips when he called my $50,000 bet and I put him on a small pair and a straight draw after the flop of 4,6,7 rainbow. I had 6,9 and knew that my sixes were the best hand.

If I get on TV, will I be famous?

You're already famous because of my cartoon.

Focus on opportunities to increase your chip position and be diligent in protecting yourself from losing even one of them.

Because of his demeanor when he called my bet, my instincts told me that my sixes were the best hand on the flop. When a king came on the turn, I wanted to force him to either call as many chips as I had so he would release his hand or to call my bet and be at a disadvantage. I never expected him to have K,5 giving him a higher pair than mine. It cost me an opportunity to win the tournament.

If I just win $1 million, that will be enough.

Start with $2 million and I am sure you will get there.

> Thy words I grant are bigger; for I wear not my dagger in my mouth.
>
> **WILLIAM SHAKESPEARE**

> Never engage a dagger, go about your own business and let it rot off the vine.
>
> **CHARLIE SHOTEN**

Frankly, I was a little overconfident and did not take the time to reconsider that he could have a king in his hand. I didn't have to go all in after he raised my $100,000 bet on the turn, nor to act so soon. When all of your chips are on the line, take an especially long time to consider and reconsider the gain and benefit of your action. Just the fact that I was risking all of my chips on this hand should have been enough to stop me from re-raising him all in. After so many hours and days of play, it is a real challenge for anyone to maintain focus and take the time to consider all

My mother-in-law won't give me any more money. She says she's broke.

Get divorced and remarry.

the possible consequences of any action. In No-Limit Hold'em, any thoughtless act or distraction during the long hours of play can cost you the tournament.

In summary, two primary factors that separate the great players from the average ones are:

- Intuition
- Estimates of the implied odds in each hand

This is where the ability to maintain focus is most important. Distractions (TT) of any kind will not allow these two essential skills to help you play the game at its highest levels. To be dominant, active and aggressive, your sixth sense must be turned on and alert. You must be aware of every nuance at the table and every response to your actions. You cannot allow your focus to weaken or wander away from the essential information you need to know. ♣

I know myself and stay in my comfort zone. What is wrong with that?

You only live once.

Ten Commitments in Play

1   **MY ATTITUDE IS GRATITUDE.**
   - ~   *I am grateful for being healthy and being able to afford my buy-in.*
   - ~   *My family is safe and well cared for.*
   - ~   *I appreciate my knowledge and ability.*

2   **I FOCUS ON MY INNER SELF AND LOOK AFTER IT AND CARE FOR IT.**
   - ~   *I appreciate myself and am kind to myself and others.*

3   **I NOTICE ANY HARMFUL MEMORY, THOUGHT, IDEA OR BELIEF I AM HOLDING.**
   - ~   *If it causes distress, distractions or harm to me, I use my next Commitment to let go of it.*

4   **I HOLD MY INTENTIONS TO LET GO OF TT AND NOT BE ATTACHED TO THEM.**
   - ~   *I am aware they might destroy my chance to do well in tournaments.*
   - ~   *I am especially vigilant at this time.*

5   **I BELIEVE AND TRUST IN MYSELF.**
   - ~   *I rely on my internal forces to help me let go of TT.*
   - ~   *I am relaxed and do not give them another thought.*

6 I AM CALM, CONFIDENT AND CLEAR, AND I WAIT FOR MY BEST CHOICE TO APPEAR.

~ *I consider all of my choices and their potential consequences.*

~ *It may take time, but my best choice will appear with regularity.*

7 I AM NOT ATTACHED TO OUTCOME.

~ *I keep an open mind and welcome any result.*

~ *I look for the gold nugget in any outcome and treat it as an opportunity to learn and grow as a player.*

8 I HUMBLY ASK FOR FORGIVENESS.

~ *I request forgiveness from those I knowingly or unknowingly neglected or abused through my thoughts, words or deeds.*

~ *I humbly grant forgiveness to those who knowingly or unknowingly neglected or abused me through their thoughts, words or deeds.*

9 I NOTICE THE NEXT TT WHEN IT APPEARS AND REPEAT COMMITMENTS #3 THROUGH #8.

10 I MAINTAIN MY ATTITUDE OF GRATITUDE.

~ *I'm grateful – especially through every bad beat.*

Sixth Commitment

A VERY INTERESTING HAND came up at the 2003 World Poker Tour at Foxwood Casino in Connecticut that demonstrates how I use my Sixth Commitment during a tournament.

> How absolute the knave is,
> We must speak by the card, or
> equivocation will undo us.
>
> **WILLIAM SHAKESPEARE**

> The cards never lie.
>
> **CHARLIE SHOTEN**

This hand occurred during the first day of the tournament. It is particularly interesting because it happened between Greg Raymer and me before he won the 2004 World Series of Poker main event – and $5 million! I had forgotten about this hand and was reminded of it when I sat at a table with him again at the 2004 Foxwood tournament. Greg brought it up and complimented me on it.

Greg was playing very aggressively and had doubled his chip stack to $20,000. I was struggling with the same $10,000 chips I started with. The blinds were $100-200 with a $25 ante. Greg was in the first seat across from me in the fifth seat when he raised two times the big blind as I looked at pocket sevens.

I repeated in my mind, "I am calm, confident and clear, and wait for my best choice to appear after considering all of my choices and the consequences of each."

When will I win a gold bracelet at the World Series of Poker?

When you stop trying to win, let go of the TT that are sabotaging your game and life and see in the mirror that radiant contagious smile I talk about so much.

My goal is to make lots of money. Why should I buy your book?

Because you are broke and in debt.

One other player called in front of me. I considered raising Greg to find out if he was slow-playing a big pocket pair. Considering my smaller stack of chips and it being the first day of the tournament, I chose to just call and wait to see the flop and his reaction to it. If I hit a set, the implied odds certainly justified the call. And if small cards flopped, I could have an excellent chance of having the best hand or outplaying the other players.

There was $2350 in the pot. The flop showed A,7,3 rainbow. Because Greg's original raise was only two times the big blind, I was immediately concerned that he might be slow-playing pocket aces.

Greg then made a very small bet of $600. This increased my concern about the strength of his hand. There was only one hand he could have that would knock me out of the tournament and I wanted to take every possible precaution to protect myself. I was holding my Sixth Commitment at the forefront of my attention like a threatened cat with my hair standing up (figuratively). Because my hand was so strong, I was projecting a weak image. This would also protect me from a large bet on the river if he really had the aces.

> Such bugs and goblins in my life.
>
> **WILLIAM SHAKESPEARE**

> Now we know what to do with them, Bill. Let go of them. Let go of them. Let go of them.
>
> **CHARLIE SHOTEN**

> Brevity is the soul of wit,
> And tediousness the limbs
> and outward flourishes.
>
> **WILLIAM SHAKESPEARE**

> Less is more where wit is
> concerned as deleting what
> you are not is more where
> you are concerned.
>
> **CHARLIE SHOTEN**

The turn card was a 5. The board now showed A,7,3,5 rainbow so that only a set of aces or a 4,6 straight could beat me. Greg made a substantial bet of $2000. I felt that he had the nuts and wanted me to call. I decided that if I raised him $3000 – not $2500 or $2000 – it would tell me for sure if he really had me beat. At that point, if I had just called him, I would probably be faced with an all-in bet on the river and have to call with my set of sevens. He immediately went all-in over the top of my bet and I turned over my set of sevens and said, "Nice hand...you win." He then showed his 4,6 of spades (straight) and replied, "Now I know why you win so many tournaments."

My Ten Commitments are always at the forefront of my mind and working for me in every way possible. They create a joyous mindset, keep all doubts and fears from affecting my play, and save my strength during the long hours of play by letting go of all distractions that do not contribute to my success and that sabotage my game. ◆

Thank God for you. You have saved me.

You're confusing me with another guy.

Top (left to right) — Scotty Nguyen, Charlie & Joe Smith Jr., Carlos Mortensen
Middle row — Minh Nguyen, Kathy Liebert, Felicia Lee, Roxci Rhodes
Bottom row — Greg Raymer, Jimmy Miller, "Miami" John Cernuto & Charlie

No-Limit Hold'em Overview

THERE ARE SIX WAYS to play a hand. All the pros are aware of these strategies. They can be used individually and in combinations to fit different situations.

1 Play your **CARDS**
2 Play your **POSITION**
3 Play the **BOARD**
4 Play the **MONEY**
5 Play the **PLAYER**
6 **BLUFF**

These open you to a broader vision of your play. When making critical choices, they help you understand the thinking of the better players at the table.

My memories, ideas, thoughts and beliefs have made me who and what I am. How can I give them up?

Choose the ones that cause you stress and sell them to some fool who finds them valuable and will pay you a big price for them.

Example A:
Play the Money, the Board, Your Position and Bluff

$2000 is in the pot before the flop. You are first to act and you have a 2,9 off-suit mediocre hand or worse. You bet $2100 on the flop because you feel that no one hit that flop and there is a 50/50 chance that the players behind you will fold. You only need to be right 50% of the time to break even. This play may cause other players to call you when you have an exceptionally strong hand and you make the same aggressive bet after the flop. These are the implied odds that you are looking for with this type of bet. This image at the table can do wonders for your chip stack.

I make so much money that I must be okay. I can go anywhere and do anything I want. What can your book offer me?

If you notice your Thought Terrorists and let them go, you will enjoy being where you are.

Example B:
Play the Player and Bluff

Notice which players at the table you feel are predictable. See the flop whenever you can get heads-up with any small call and any reasonable hand. You won't need to have the best hand most of the time to win the pot and you can get away from any hand very fast.

Again, don't expect to win any tournaments playing only the cards you are dealt. How you play your cards, along with the five other ways to play a hand, will make the critical difference. Be willing to gamble or find another pastime. ♥

We must not cease from exploration and the end of all our exploring will be to arrive where we began for the first time.

T.S. ELLIOT

The Great Wall of Charlie

Noticing Thought Terrorists During a Tournament

DURING THE MANY HOURS of a poker tournament, I am always alert to any thoughts that distract me from the action at the table and weaken my focus. Worries and doubts are good examples. I focus on them, notice the harm they do to my game and let go of them. They are a cold slap in the face that wake me up and help me refocus on the game. If I don't take them seriously, they make me lose every time; so I let go of them and am no longer distracted. As long as I follow my Ten Commitments, these Thought Terrorists cannot affect my mindset or my play.

TT, such as judgments, comparisons, expectations, doubts and beliefs about myself and other players, no longer cloud my decision-making process. Other TT, such as worrying about the rent, thinking about my health or fantasizing about winning the tournament, also have no effect on my decisions. The list goes on and on.

Not being distracted is what separates the truly great players from the rest of the field. I always study the most successful players. Often I see a friendly smile, an aura of confidence, a joyous and patient mindset, an aggressive stance and a dominant, yet peaceful presence. Distractions do not effect them.

My Roadmap keeps my Ten Commitments at the forefront of my mind where any hurtful memory,

If I lose my rent, where can I find a good game to win it back?

On the street where you sleep.

thought, idea or belief that arises must get past my "Great Wall of Charlie" (Ten Commitments). If fear shows itself, I notice the thoughts that cause it – such as doubts about my abilities – and my Ten Commitments, supported by my joyous mindset, will help me let go of all my doubts. The fear will vanish and no longer affect my play.

Can I promote your roadmap everywhere I go?

Only when your contagious radiant smile appears.

My mindset always keeps me aware of the need to maintain my focus throughout the long hours of a tournament. In the past, at critical moments when I needed to exercise the strictest discernment, I sometimes found myself acting impulsively and abandoning all caution. I was frequently tired in those moments and some force beyond me moved my chips into the center of the pot. Looking back, usually immediately, I was able to see the mindlessness of my action as if someone else had taken over and played the hand for me.

> What should such fellows as (he) do crawling between earth and heaven.
>
> **WILLIAM SHAKESPEARE**

> Surrender and let go of. He has disappeared and only his destructive thoughts, ideas, beliefs and memories can still be seen.
>
> **CHARLIE SHOTEN**

At times I sat on my fingers to keep from acting too soon, but at other times I just forgot to do this although I was aware of the problem. Where did I go when "someone other than me" acted too soon? I would never have made those bad choices had I been calm, clear and present. Later I would go over again and again in my mind the particular play that knocked me out of that tournament.

> In nature there's no blemish
> but the mind; none
> can be called deformed
> but the unkind.
>
> **WILLIAM SHAKESPEARE**

> My mind, my mind, my mind,
> that is the matter with me.
>
> **CHARLIE SHOTEN**

For days I would be angry with myself and have my hands around my throat. Believe me, that feeling hurt and I found it impossible to forgive myself and let go of it.

Now, with my Ten Commitments to protect and guide me, that happens very rarely, if at all. Those bad feelings were an obstacle to my happiness and success on and off the poker table. No wonder it took me until age 65 to find my Roadmap of my Ten Commitments and to let go of TT and free myself from their wrath. I hope others can take advantage and follow the path I have walked to free themselves from their TT without waiting as many years as I had to.

At that time, the bad beats I endured from bad luck never bothered me for long. It was only those times that I did something really stupid that I would never in a millions years have done if I had been calm, confident and clear.

Freedom is a two-edged sword. It might create too many possibilities.

You can always fall on your sword.

The biggest reason I was so hard on myself was that I had done this many times before. I knew that it was hurting my game and it still continued to happen.

A few issues I can now identify: 1) I should have known better after all the times I had done this (I gave myself a strong scolding for that one);

Be willing to gamble or find another pastime.

2) My lack of kindness to myself when my ego kept telling me that I was too smart to act so dumb; and 3) My Thought Terrorists had their way with me.

> One may smile. And smile and still be a villain.
>
> **WILLIAM SHAKESPEARE**

> A radiant contagious smile cannot belong to any villain. Just your ordinary smile.
>
> **CHARLIE SHOTEN**

I had played right into the hand of TT I was harboring and did not even know their names, where they lived or how to let go of them. I was like a punch-drunk fighter, striking out at some phantom or vampire that was sucking out my life force and leaving me helpless.

Let's look at an actual hand where I gave myself a hard time and see what I would do now. At a Bellagio tournament with a big prize pool, I was in a very competitive chip position. "Someone other than the real me" played out my hand. The real me never would have made the choices that other me made.

I looked at two red aces and limped under the gun (first to act after the blinds). Four other players called and the flop showed 2,3,5 rainbow. I was second to act and made a fairly large bet (1-1/2 times the pot) that one player called. I immediately put him on a set (three of a kind) or a small pair and a straight draw. I decided to lay down my hand if he raised my next bet. The turn card was a 6. I made another large bet and he made a substantial raise. Before I realized what I had done,

Why do my bad beats hurt so bad?

Because they happen to you.

I called him, throwing all caution to the wind by ignoring my first decision. I knew for sure he had a set or had made the straight. On the river, as luck would have it, my third ace came. First to bet, I went all in. He called me and showed his two fours for the straight.

This was a time when I could have used my Roadmap of Ten Commitments. I desperately wanted to eliminate such compulsive poor play from my mindset so it would never happen again, as well as get rid of the TT causing me such agony and stress.

Can I torture my Thought Terrorists before I let them go?

No. The ACLU will sue you for all your money.

The Commitments that could have helped me the most were 2, 3, 4, 6 and 8: Focus, Notice, Intentions, Appear and Forgiveness. Now I would remain calm, confident and clear and my intentions would help me let go of those TT and free myself. I am not overstating this because I was truly tormented by those self-defiling TT. The flow of my life was disrupted and the stress that was caused, if continued, would not only hurt my poker game, but could cause future destructive behaviors, such as poor eating habits, loss of sleep and mental and physical dis-ease.

> (You) vicious mole of nature!
>
> **WILLIAM SHAKESPEARE**

> All Thought Terrorists take heed, we are on to you.
>
> **CHARLIE SHOTEN**

My Great Wall of Charlie and my Roadmap of Ten Commitments always help me let go of all TT I can find and identify that are causing my mindset to suffer stress or any resistance to my natural flow of life. It is simple and can be walked by anyone.

It's important to understand that hurtful memories, thoughts, beliefs and ideas you hold onto are not part of you or connected to you in any way.

YOU hold onto THEM. They are parasitic vermin killing you slowly, not with a kiss, but with a vicious appetite for your life's blood. They don't have anything to gain because when they finally kill you, they die along with you unless you have passed them on to your children.

> (His) tongue out venoms all the worms of Nile.
>
> **WILLIAM SHAKESPEARE**

> The thoughts that cause doubt and fear we hear in our ear.
>
> **CHARLIE SHOTEN**

Use my Ten Commitments to help you let go of any thoughts that cause you stress. It is time to Focus, Notice and Let Go Of. Our future depends upon each of us taking a stand in this critical conflict. The stakes are high and affect all of us, especially children. Hopefully our current business leaders, teachers and politicians will alert us to the danger we are facing and will actively assist us in any way they can. We shouldn't listen to the chatter of those only interested in their own power and agendas. TT control them. ♠

If I get a big high every time I let go of a Thought Terrorist, won't the government step in and make it illegal?

After the next election I will let you know.

Let's do all we can to better the experience of everyone connected with the game.

A Pro's Reaction

VINCE BURGIO

IT TOOK ME A LITTLE WHILE to grasp what Charlie was talking about when he said we should have less expectations. At first, I took this to mean that one shouldn't have a positive attitude or outlook. This, I thought, was something I didn't want to buy into. Only after listening and giving it some thought, did I really understand what he meant by having less expectations.

We all have certain expectations that allow us to lead our lives without a minimum of stress. These basic expectations allow us to plan for the future and have orderly lives. So Charlie is certainly not advocating that we walk around expecting that we're not going to wake up tomorrow.

What I think he is telling us is that we should not waste time and energy with thinking about what we expect in most situations. It means we are more or less devoid of the thoughts accompanying whether we do or do not accomplish something – whether something does or doesn't happen.

We should do our very best to have every situation or circumstance unfold or come out as we want it to. We should use all of our energy to accomplish this mission. Whether or not we actually succeed is not the most important thing; what is important ultimately is that we do the best we can and that we do not let ourselves be distracted with goals or expectations.

Let's apply this concept to playing in a poker tournament.

We start out with high hopes and great expectations. On the days when everything goes well, we arrive at the end of the tournament convinced that our positive expectations played a role in our success. That is fine and if everyday we went into a tournament with expectations and we succeeded, we would all know that the key to winning was just having these expectations. But we know that's not the way it goes. Most of the time, we end up walking out not having our expectations met. This, according to Charlie, and now to me, is a more damaging than helpful attitude – a burden we are better off not having to carry.

This, you must understand, does not mean that you should go into any situation with negative expectations. It is easy to see that this would not be helpful if we are hoping to succeed but expecting to fail.

Therein lies the whole point of Charlie's notion: that expectations get in our way and, in many cases, cause us to lose focus and lose energy when something we expect to happen does not.

Here's an example of what happens when we put too much emphasis on expectations. Let's say you're playing No-Limit Hold'em and you pick up two aces against another player. The money goes all in before the flop. You turn over two aces and your opponent turns over seven/deuce. You have high expectations of winning this hand. When you don't, it is easy to allow this to carry over into your play, assuming you didn't get knocked out of the tournament on that hand.

Since adopting Charlie's advice, I have trained myself to not think about what the outcome should be, but rather watch it as I might watch a movie unfold. When it is over, I accept it and just go on to the next moment in time. ♠

My Challenge to the Poker Community

GAMBLING IS A PART OF POKER, but not all poker is gambling. We can distinguish poker from gambling because it is now a popular spectator sport and winning requires skill. Poker also offers opportunities that other gambling games do not. Pulling a lever or betting on a number at a roulette wheel involves little expertise. All is left to chance. Winning at poker, on the other hand, requires great expertise, experience and skills in personal relationships, as well as math. The interactions between poker players are an important part of the game, make for good TV entertainment and offer an opportunity for the evolution and growth of each player. Staying focused at the table is necessary to reach the best decisions and makes the game of poker a highly skilled enterprise. The focused player also reflects an aura of dominance and thereby has a big advantage.

> Love sought is good, but given unsought is better.
>
> **WILLIAM SHAKESPEARE**

> The beauty of love given is the experience of love returned.
>
> **CHARLIE SHOTEN**

Individuals and companies profiting from poker can support the poker community by contributing facilities and personnel to spread the message of *NO-LIMIT LIFE*. The entire poker community and its environment can become a bright light for young and old alike. Players, dealers, management, service people and spectators can enjoy the support of all who become aware of their TT and how my Ten Commitments can help them let go of them.

I never thought much about the blessings of being human.

It is the main thing you should be grateful for. See Commitments 1 and 10.

Imagine the poker environment becoming home to radiant contagious smiles spreading like wildfire throughout the entire poker community where all are welcome and supported by each other. We can change the world by setting an example of what is possible, especially as poker is now in the spotlight on national television and growing in popularity around the globe.

I am already over 50. Isn't it too late for me to change?

I am never talking about changing. I am talking about becoming who you already are.

Something must be done to change the direction of centuries of man's inhumanity to man brought about by man's Thought Terrorists. Only those who are prisoners of their TT become evil despots. Humans free from TT would never do such horrendous things.

My vision of the support we can make available includes sharing each other's experiences when dealing with our TT and discussing what we are doing about them. We can spread our message through television tournament productions, breakfast meetings, seminars, workshops, chat rooms and live poker events (similar to tennis, golf, theater and TV productions). Let's get the word out about Thought Terrorists – where they hide and how they slowly destroy our immune systems, cause destructive behaviors, etc. – and how we are letting go of them.

Let's share our newfound strengths everywhere. Yes, we can get better. We can free ourselves. We can support each other. We can all wear radiant contagious smiles more of the time. Not a bad result...and quite a magnet for attracting new members to our poker community and keeping old ones. ♠

The Greatest Gift

For the Children of the World – the Best Parents Possible

I MAGINE LOVING PARENTS who hold no judgments, resentments, anger, jealousy, frustration, depression, resignations, expectations, etc.; whose memories, thoughts, ideas and beliefs that create stress are banned from their being; who are open vessels with clear, confident, and compassionate outlooks on life. I hope the meaning and significance of this is clear. Even more important is the belief that we can work towards this goal and make meaningful progress in this direction.

Thought Terrorists offer us nothing of value. They do not grow wheat, write books or invent anything important for the human race. They just feed off those who create the sustenance of human life. If we recognize what and where they are and the damage they do to our lives, we can notice them and let go of them. They cannot exist without our supporting, nurturing and holding onto them.

Take a new look at your old beliefs. What I am proposing has always seemed difficult and impossible to accomplish because we have never had my Ten Commitments to follow and use as a tool to help us let go of our TT.

How can I bring a new life into this awful world we live in?

Start with letting go of all the awful thoughts you are holding about our world.

These Commitments can revolutionize how we handle our TT, which we created as an antidote to heal the emotional wounds we hold onto from when we were hurt or abused in our past. We created our TT and we can let go of them.

TT reside within each of us and they hold only a fierce threat with no substance. For me personally, the game is over. I notice them, focus my intentions and choose to let go of them. How much simpler can it get? I will repeat it over and over again because it is the most important exercise I can do for myself and for the good of my family. How can I ever be bored again when I still have TT to notice and let go of? Do you think it is more interesting, fun or important to watch television for hours a day?

Is professional poker a good profession for my kid to aspire to?

Only if you can afford the tuition.

Wake up and take your life back. If you are not becoming less of what you are not (letting go of TT), you are not being who you really are, meaning something else is living and controlling your life. You may have sensed, like I have ever since I can remember, that you were more of what you were NOT than who you were. Each TT that you hold onto makes you that much more of what you are not. It is a living agony to know that and to try with all your heart to change it, but not know how and to be left all alone with no tools to free yourself from them.

> He who joyfully marches in rank and file has already earned my contempt. He has been given a large brain by mistake, since for him the spinal cord would suffice.
>
> **ALBERT EINSTEIN**

> You are referring to the goose step march of the Nazi soldiers, Albert. I agree. It takes a MOTHER and FATHER to raise a child, NOT A VILLAGE!
>
> **CHARLIE SHOTEN**

Looking back before my Ten Commitments, all the efforts I made to free myself only created more TT. I don't regret the lost opportunities of the first 65 years of my life because I use my Ten Commitments

24/7 to help me keep letting go of my TT and keep me present. Why would anyone want to harbor harmful thoughts when it is so simple and easy to let them go? My Commitments are a mantra that repeats with little effort even when I sleep.

> Either you stay in the shallow end of the pool or you go in the ocean.
>
> **CHRISTOPHER REEVES**

Memorize my Ten Commitments and put them in the forefront of your mind. And as your own mind control, use this mantra to help you let go of all hurtful memories, thoughts, ideas and beliefs.

If you do not let go of your TT, you will pass them onto your children. TT are contagious and will infect all your relationships like a virus. They hurt you, your children and your poker game. Once you let go of your TT, you will see your children in a new way and you will be highly motivated to help protect your children from their Thought Terrorists.

What do I gain after winning at poker besides money?

Quality time with your family I hope.

Once parents focus on noticing and letting go of their TT, they will be able to help their children focus, notice and let go of them. Teaching children to do this will be the best present they give them. Imagine a family where everyone at the dinner table has a joyous mind-set and a radiant contagious smile. Why not reach for it? LET GO OF YOUR TT! ♠

*Why would anyone want
to harbor harmful thoughts
when it is so simple and
easy to let go of them?*

In Conclusion

WHILE WRITING THIS BOOK, I came to a deeper understanding of the ideas and concepts expressed in it. They still surprise and amaze me. They are a gift I will embrace and enjoy for the rest of my life. I never realized that I could write a book, create fun cartoons to illustrate my points or use Wm. Shakespeare to give my ideas more credibility and make them more comprehensible. I never imagined that I would discover my Ten Commitments which would protect, guide and liberate me from the TT that have sabotaged my life for as long as I can remember. I did not foresee the effect my personal freedom would have on my daughter, grandchildren, sister and friends, or the ripple effect my Roadmap to my Ten Commitments would have on all who are touched by them.

> Thou art sensible in nothing but blows, and so is an ass.
>
> **WILLIAM SHAKESPEARE**

> As an ass blows, head for the hills.
>
> **CHARLIE SHOTEN**

How could you ever be bored again if you become a 24/7 Thought Terrorist Hunter? Each TT you notice and let go of allows you to reach a little higher and run a little faster in every area of your life.

The dark cell in which you have allowed destructive feelings to hold you prisoner will be demolished one TT at a time. When the feeling of resentment, for example, is no longer poisoning your mind and your life, the freedom you feel will allow you to be more of who you really are. You will then make choices that come from your instincts and true passions.

I now know that what I see through my eyes is probably distorted. How can I see more clearly what is really there?

Let go of...
Let go of...
Let go of...
and Let go
of again.

Few have seemed to do better by taking your advice, I need a guarantee. I haven't won a tournament in five years.

I'll give you a five-year guarantee.

And most amazing of all, you will at last be able to achieve your deepest hopes and highest dreams. This prison break will make escaping from Alcatraz seem like a picnic!

As TT, like doubt, are released, your freedom from them will feel like a bigger poker tournament win than you could ever imagine. I am experiencing this at the ripe young age of 68. I used to feel like I was fighting my way out of a paper bag until just a few years ago. I am not bashful to share this with you or concerned that I might come off as reaching. It is what I am experiencing being who I really am.

I hope many will support and help me spread my vision of health, happiness and personal freedom to the far reaches of our worldly community. I wholeheartedly believe that less is more and that more tools and books with more pages to sell will take away from our goal: being less of what we are not and seeing who we really are and the release of our inherent creativity. "Keep it simple, stupid" sounds better to me. Personal freedom for those of us who crave it is just an intention and a mindset away.

With love and best wishes,

Charlie ❤

You talk so crazy... about Thought Terrorists, becoming more or less. Why did I buy your book? I'm so confused.

So am I.

Everything You Need to Know About Poker

If you want to find out more about the game of Poker, here are online resources that will provide everything you need to know. Charlie's home on the internet is **nolimitlife.net** which links to "Charlie's Corner" on some of these sites.

Lasvegasvegas.com *The jump-off point to all the other poker content on this site, this page contains the newest site content additions and a complete list of poker resources including:*

> **Poker Blog**
> **Poker Blog/Strategy**
> **Professional Poker Biographies**
> **Robert's Rules of Poker (Version 5)**
> **Las Vegas Tournament Locator**
> **Poker Links** *PokerPlayerNewspaper.com*
> **Photo Galleries** *Hundreds of Photos of Pros and Big Tournaments*
> **Much More Poker**

Cardplayer.com *The #1 Poker Authority features:*

> **Card Player Magazine** *Current Issues and Online Archive of CP Magazine Articles*
> **Tournament Coverage** *Live Updates, Reports and Analysis, Streaming Video from the World Poker Tour and the World Series of Poker*
> **Poker Tools** *Poker School, Free Poker, Rules of Poker, Poker Odds Calculator*
> **Poker Media** *Poker on TV, Larry Grossman Show, Poker News, Newsletters*
> **My Cardplayer** *Web Mail, Poker Analyst, Customized Homepages, Forums*
> **Poker Rooms** *Listings*
> **Poker Extras** *Poker & the Law, Poker E-Cards, Opinion Polls, Cartoon of the Day,*
> **Shop OnLine**
> **Much More Poker**

International Poker Association

As a founding member of this international not-for-profit organization, I strongly recommend that all those involved in the poker community join and support the growth of the Association for the benefit of all. Thanks to David Chiu, professional player, and Maureen Brooks, IPA President, for their commitment to see that the Association works tirelessly to address the needs of the players, the game, the industry and the fans. The Association will recognize and maximize opportunities presented to the poker community and all related industries.

PURPOSE STATEMENT: To advance and advocate the interests and rights of poker players everywhere. Careful negotiations with outside opportunities in cooperation with players will ensure that players are protected in all aspects of poker and business.

1   Advance the interest of poker players
2   Advocate for the rights of poker players
3   Standardize the rules of the game of poker
4   Maintain a comprehensive ranking system
5   Stay in constant contact with the poker community
6   Open business negotiations with key sponsors and endorsements
7   Control group licensing opportunities within the Association guidelines
8   Group franchise and health insurance programs

MISSION STATEMENT: The IPA is a not-for-profit organization that promotes the game of poker while continuing to enhance the standards of the profession. It is comprised of professional, semi-professional and recreational players who, along with fans and sponsors of tournament poker, are dedicated to growing participation in the game of poker worldwide and strive to continually increase its marketability.

For more information: www.ipapoker.com or call (303) 825-8700.

My Personal Milestone Books

Here are the books that put me on the path
to writing this book:

♥ *The Celestine Prophesy*
James Redfield (Warner Books Inc.)

♥ *Why Is This Happening to Me...Again?*
And What You Can Do About It
Michael Ryce, M.D. (self-published)

♥ *Conversations with God*
Neale Donald Walsch (G.P. Putnam's Sons)

♥ *Letter to Earth: Who We Are Becoming...What We Need to Know*
Elia Wise (Random House/Harmony Books)

♥ *Self I-Dentity through HO'OPONOPONO*
The Foundation of I, Inc. (www.hooponopono.org)

A special thanks to William Shakespeare,
the greatest Thought Terrorist Hunter
in the history of mankind.

> (His) ambition swell'd so much
> that it did almost stretch
> the sides o' th' world.
> **WILLIAM SHAKESPEARE**

> (His) TT are all that
> is left of him.
> **CHARLIE SHOTEN**

Credits

Thanks to Nita Alvarez and everyone at The Alvarez Group Inc. in Los Angeles. Graphic designer *extraordinaire,* Nita understood my vision and worked closely with me as creative muse and editor to bring my words (and Guru Charlie) to these pages.

Thanks to Pamela Shandel, of Las Vegas and Paris, France, for her uniquely artistic perspective of the game as a player, dealer and international photographer – and for capturing my radiant contagious smile. With assistance from card magician, Chris Mastellone, and chip facilitator, Jason Newsom, Pamela's images grace the front cover, back cover, inside front and back cover and pages 7, 19, 23, 27, 35, 39, 49, 65, 67, 75 and 109.

Thanks to Joe Smith, brilliant webmaster of *lasvegasvegas.com*, and his dad, Joe Smith, Sr., expert on-the-scene around-town photographer, for their generous time and support – and especially for the use of Joe Sr.'s great photos on pages 55, 71, 77, 83, 91, 97, 101 and 119.

Thanks to CardPlayer.com for the photos on page 14 and 15.

And special thanks to my unnamed colleague (you know who you are) for diligently providing excellent feedback and editing services – and for feeding me.

Much gratitude to the Mastery Circle Los Angeles, a group of friends who have been meeting every Tuesday morning since 1986 to share breakfast, enrich each other's lives and encourage the development of projects like *NO-LIMIT LIFE*. For information on this organization, visit their website at *www.masterycirclelosangeles.org*.

Glossary

Basic terminology for those who are not familiar with poker...yet.

All-In	To bet all the money you have on the table
Ante	A small bet/chip all players pay before a hand is dealt
Bad Beat	A odds-favored hand defeated by a River card
Blind	A forced bet to open the pot; usually in lieu of an ante
Board	Community cards dealt face up in the center of the table
Bluff	A bet or raise to steal a pot with the worst hand
Buy-In	Amount required to enter a poker game or tournament
Card-Dead	Player being dealt bad cards for a long time
Call	To match a bet; not fold or raise
Chips	Round tokens represent cash based on color
Drawing Hand	Need another card to have a good hand
Final Table	Last table in a tournament where winner is decided
Flop	First three community cards dealt face up in Hold'em
Fold	Decline to call a bet, thus dropping out of a hand
Gold Bracelet	Top prize of every World Series of Poker Tournament
Limp	Call the blind before the flop; not raise or call a raise
Loose play	Enter many pots

Nuts	Best possible hand
No-Limit	Game where players can wager any/all chips in one bet
Pat Hand	Holding or being dealt a complete hand
Pass	Decline to bet
Position	Location in the betting sequence relative to the players still in the hand
Pot	Total amount of money or chips bet in any hand
Rainbow	Cards of different suits
River	The last face-up card to complete all hands
Royal Flush	Highest-rated hand in poker
Raise	To bet double or more than a preceding player; "bump"
Satellite	A small tournament with prize of a seat in a larger tournament
Set	Three of a kind; in Hold'em, a pair in your hand with one on the board
Showdown	Point at the end of play when the pot is awarded to winner(s)
Slowplay	To play unaggressively with a very strong hand
Stack	Amount/stack of chips a player has on the table
Tight Play	Enter fewer pots

Contact Charlie

I welcome your input, comments and ideas and look forward to working together to set each of us free – one player at a time! Write or email any results you have experienced after reading *NO-LIMIT LIFE* that you wish to share.

CHARLIE SHOTEN

Post Office Box 34298

Las Vegas, Nevada 89133

charlieshoten@msn.com

COPY this page to order additional books for your family and friends.

Please send me _____ books at $30 each plus $5 shipping & handling.

Name_____

Address_____

City_____State_____ Zip_____

Telephone (   )_____ Fax (   )_____

Email_____

Payment: *Send a money order payable to Charlie Shoten (address shown above) for the total amount $_____ OR complete below to charge to your VISA or MasterCard.*

☐ *VISA*   ☐ *MASTERCARD*

Card Number_____

Exp. Date (mo/yr)_____ SIGNATURE_____

Attention Corporations / Business Owners   Contact Charlie to CUSTOMIZE this book with your logo and/or message as a promotional item or gift for employees, clients and customers.

*We look forward
to working together
to set each of us free —
one player at a time!*

119

NOW

WE ARE

SET FREE.

WE ARE

THE BEST

WE CAN BE.

♥ ♣ ♦ ♠